# THE DIRTY TRUTH

## George W. Bush's Oil and Chemical Dependency

### How He Sold Out Texans

### and the Environment

### To Big Business Polluters

By Rick Abraham

*Forward by Terry O'Rourke*

WITHDRAWN FROM COLLECTION

Copyright © Mainstream Publishers, 2000

ISBN 0-9705190-0-1

All Rights Reserved
P.O. Box 7635
Houston Texas 77270

Cover Photo of Exxon facility
Baytown, Texas by Peter Altman

# Acknowledgments

The author wishes to thank John O'Connor and Carolyn Mugar for helping to make this book possible and for supporting environmental protection efforts in Texas for over a decade. Houston attorney Valorie Davenport made significant contributions to this book and Karen Spencer assisted with editing. Special appreciation is expressed to the many individuals and organizations who contributed by virtue of their research, reports, articles, and hard work.

Valorie Davenport, like Terry O'Rourke, was a key player in some of the case histories cited in the following pages. Her role as an attorney representing pollution victims and industry whistle–blowers, and as a mother concerned about the health and welfare of her family, has provided valuable insight and perspective. The same thirst for justice that motivated her to be a Republican candidate for the Texas Supreme Court also motivated her to contribute to this book and tell a story that needs to be told.

The author also wishes to thank Jim Baldauf, the citizen activist and Texas oil-man. More than just a communications expert, Jim has been an inspiration and a loyal friend to the environment. Jim, like Valorie, Terry, and all those making up the citizen organizations referenced in this book, are determined foes of those who would trample our earth and our rights. They understand that the "personal responsibility" George W. Bush so often mentions, includes a "social responsibility" to protect our environment and the welfare of others.

APR 0 4 2002

# About the Author

Since 1988 Rick Abraham has served as Director of Texans United Education Fund, a non-profit and non-partisan environmental organization started with the help of country western singer and songwriter Willie Nelson and his daughter Lana Nelson.

Before working for Texans United, Rick served as the Hazardous Waste Project Director for the Texas Center for Policy Studies and the Southern Regional Organizer for the National Toxics Campaign. Over the last fifteen years he has worked throughout Texas and other states, providing organizing and technical assistance to communities with pollution problems. This work carried him to the homes of pollution victims, the state legislature and the halls of the U.S. Congress where he has testified on important environmental issues.

Rick Abraham's efforts on behalf of the environment have also carried him into federal and state courts to confront powerful corporate pollution violators like Exxon and Crown Central Petroleum. When companies have wanted to be cleaner and accountable to the public, he has negotiated precedent-setting "good neighbor" agreements, including one with the Rhone Poulenc chemical plant in Houston.

Texans United Education Fund has never been funded by industry or government and, like Abraham, it has taken a non-partisan approach to addressing the nation's environmental problems. This approach has involved educating, and when necessary, challenging public officials of all political parties.

This book relies heavily on the research of other Texas environmental and public interest organizations that serve as watchdogs and advocates for the public. These organizations and the sources of their information are identified at the end of the book. No funds from Texans United Education Fund were used in the writing or publishing of this book.

# CONTENTS

FORWARD

## A Law Enforcement Perspective on
## George W. Bush and the Environment

As a former environmental law enforcement officer, I commend Rick Abraham for laying out the facts of the Texas State government's failure to protect its citizens from industrial pollution, air toxins and hazardous wastes. Most importantly he and others explain the connections of key government environmental policy decisions and the flow of money to the Governor of Texas from powerful polluters. It is not a pretty picture.

After serving as a Texas Assistant Attorney General in the early 1970's, I served for more than a decade, as Senior Assistant Harris County Attorney. In the late 1990's, my primary responsibilities were suing polluters for penalties and obtaining court ordered injunctions compelling companies to clean up and comply with Texas laws. While I, and other prosecutors, won many of the court battles to hold polluters accountable, we have watched in frustration as our gains have been undermined or altogether negated by political maneuvering at the behest of the companies we fought.

My principal client was the Harris County Pollution Control Department, the lead local government law enforcement agency responsible for protecting our 3.4 million citizens, their animals, plants and property from contamination coming from the vast Houston ship channel, corridor of petro-chemical plants, oil refineries and industrial manufacturers. The Houston ship channel is the second largest port in the nation and the center of the largest petro-chemical complex in the United States.

It has been the formidable task of the Pollution Control Department to protect the public in the county that consistently leads the nation in the generation of hazardous waste and toxic air and water pollution, and waste. In 1999 we also led the nation with the worst ozone-smog problem, surpassing Los Angeles. The Department has been zealous, forceful, and honest in enforcing environmental protection laws. Almost without exception it has enjoyed the support of the county's governing body, the Commissioner's Court.

Simply stated: in protecting the environment, we have won most of the battles in the courts -- but have lost most of the battles in the state agencies that are run by political appointees. Sadly, there is almost always a trail of money and improper influence leading to bad environmental decisions and policy.

To be fair, as Rick Abraham is in his book, this situation was not created by the Republicans or by Governor George W. Bush. The power of lobbyists in the state capitol passing out campaign contributions has long permeated the Governor's office, the Legislature and the state agencies.

I was honored to serve as a Texas Assistant Attorney General in the Environmental Protection Division under the leadership of John L. Hill. In some of the first enforcement cases under the new state environmental laws [adopted to conform with federal laws] we successfully sued the big smoke stack industries and waste water polluters, amassing what were then record fines and getting court-ordered cleanups. From Hill's administration in the early 1970's to the present, with only one exception [Dan Morales], Texas Attorneys General, have consistently stood for vigorous environmental law enforcement. The sad news is that under Texas law, the Attorney General is generally limited to litigating only the environmental cases that the state agencies choose to prosecute.

Today the state's primary environmental protection agency is' the Texas Natural Resource Conservation Commission [TNRCC]. It is a super-agency created during the administration of Governor Ann Richards. But for a few exceptional cases, the TNRCC and its primary predecessor agencies [the Texas Air Control Board, the Texas Water Commission] were lackadaisical in protecting citizens from contamination and powerful polluters. In some respects the state agencies were like window dressing created by state government to comply with mandates from federal government laws, in particular the federal Clean Air Act, Water Quality Act and Solid Waste Disposal Act.

From their inception, these state agencies assumed responsibilities that the U.S. Environmental Protection Agency [EPA] would have administered directly in their absence. From the polluters' perspective, it was better to have an under-funded, ineffectual state agency that they could "work with" than have the federal EPA "on their backs." From a citizen's perspective and a local government perspective it appeared as if the tables of state government were always tilted in favor of the polluters.

From my perspective as a government prosecutor, state environmental agency conduct was dispiriting; but it got worse. When the Bush appointees took over the agency in 1995, there was a sea of change at the TNRCC. By increasingly adopting toothless regulations, weaseling on regulatory interpretations and cutting slack with permits and exceptions, the TNRCC was making pollution that was awful...lawful. Procedurally, the TNRCC embarked on a series of changes that increasingly cut itself off from significant citizen input. The agency began treating regulated industrial polluters as clients or "customers." The TNRCC went from its historical role of being ineffectual to becoming institutionally hostile to citizens and local government.

Perhaps the most illustrative case that demonstrates how it now is at the TNRCC is the case concerning discharges of billions of gallons of untreated wastewater into public waters. In 1996, the Harris County Pollution Control Department joined citizens in contending that the Exxon Refinery in Baytown [one of the nation's largest] should be prohibited from dumping chemically contaminated storm water into Buffalo Bayou and Galveston Bay. The County made the simple but forceful argument that Exxon's wastewater should be cleaned before being discharged.

What I vividly remember were Exxon's written comments to Governor Bush's political appointees who ran the state environmental agency. Exxon characterized Harris County's involvement and its technical evaluations as "meddlesome" and "intrusive." These were not off-handed comments from some low-level Exxon refinery official, they were general counsel approved, attack language. In my quarter century of legal experience with governments and regulated industries, I had never seen anything so arrogant. Exxon's arrogant language was accurately reflective of their corporate attitude. From their perspective, "the fix was in" at the state agency and they did not have to pretend to be courteous or respectful of the local government that I represented.

As I read the federal and state law and regulations, Exxon had to treat and clean its chemically contaminated storm water. Nevertheless, Governor Bush's appointees sided with Exxon. Indefatigable Rick Abraham and Texans United took the case to the federal courts and won, effectively overturning the decisions of the state agency.

In my battles as an attorney for the local government of Harris County, I frequently found myself on the same side of issues with Rick Abraham and Texans United. Harris County and Texans United fought to get the state agency to increase an administrative air pollution penalty for Crown Central Petroleum, an egregious grandfathered refinery polluter. We were together in fighting the state agency permit for the AEI industrial hazardous waste incinerator which was to be located in the center of the worst air quality zone in America. We lost and AEI was given a permit to release tons of pollution into air that was already severely polluted.

Much has been said in the media, and by Presidential candidate George W. Bush, about legislation passed under his watch concerning industrial "grandfathered" facilities that were exempted from the Texas Clean Air Act. I remember well the passage of the Texas Clean Air Act in 1970; I was in law school and worked on the staff of a Texas State Senator. America had just put men on the Moon. There was a consensus that technology would solve the problem of old factories and refineries that would or might have difficulties coming up to grade on the new clean air standards. So the grandfathered facilities exemption seemed reasonable.

Suppose we had speed limits on our roads and highways with stiff penalties for ordinary drivers, but voluntary, looser, and unenforceable speed limits for rich people who drove big old cars? It seems preposterous, doesn't it? Sadly, three decades after the grandfathered exemption was adopted, while local governments and ordinary citizens were facing major penalties for filthy, non-compliant air quality, major corporate polluters had the audacity to press Governor Bush and the TNRCC to keep the grandfathered exemption. As this book documents, they poured hundreds of thousands of dollars into Bush's campaign chest and came up with a voluntary compliance proposal. Can you imagine what this looks like from a law enforcement perspective.

Upon leaving the Harris County Attorney's office in 1997, I went into private law practice and served as the Chair of the Citizen's Panel for Clean Air in Harris County. Rick Abraham and Texans United were leaders in getting this panel to hold public hearings in Pasadena and North

Shore, areas severely affected by chronic, variable doses of chemical contamination. At the hearings I looked into the eyes of the people who suffered with the consequences of chemical contamination and I listened to their stories. I think for me that was the moment it really hit home. The grandfathered facilities stopped being equations of excessive emissions and words in a legal brief and instead became callous killing machines. Many of the witnesses in our hearings were literally dying from pollution.

Later I spoke at rallies and public demonstrations for clean air and against the continued grandfathered facilities exemptions. In front of the Governor's Mansion in Austin, I witnessed Rick Abraham and other Texans United members, a PTA mom from Dallas, and sympathetic refinery workers unlawfully arrested. Their "crime" was that they dared to peacefully carry signs connecting air pollution to the campaign contributions given to Governor Bush by major polluters.

Unfortunately, the story you are about to read is true. Fortunately, Rick Abraham has the courage and stamina to carry on the fight for a decent quality of life for all our citizens. I salute him.

Terry O'Rourke
Attorney and Counselor
Houston, Texas
August, 2000

# George W. Bush
## *The Man, The Politician, and The Money*

The truth is we don't know what George W. Bush would do as President. He would not be the first politician to promise one thing and then do another. The closest we may come to knowing what he will do, is to look at what he has done in the past as governor of the nation's second largest state. His actions, more than his words, give us insight into his values and tell us where his true loyalties lie. These are unlikely to change.

What do we really know about George W. Bush, the man? We know he began his career in the oil fields of West Texas. He "comes from oil." It's in the family. However, this was no ordinary oil field worker. George W. Bush also comes from high level, fast-moving politics. He is the fortunate son of a former CIA Director, Vice President, and then President of the United States of America. George W. Bush has been shaped by the experiences of a life and lifestyle that few people could even begin to imagine.

Having been raised on the milk of politics all his life, it is also understandable that the real substance of the man would not be readily (or accurately) revealed by how he portrays himself—or by the spin others use to portray him to the public. Like the rest of us, George W. Bush is most accurately defined by his own actions. Unlike the rest of us, his actions can directly affect millions of people's lives.

We are a nation and a world with growing environmental problems. What the next President does about these problems will make a difference in all our lives. As numerous polls have shown, people care deeply about the environment. Most of us have watched with sadness as the rivers, lakes, and landscapes of our youth have been defaced or, worse yet, destroyed. More and more citizens are discovering that they live or work down-wind or down-stream from some source of pollution. With alarming frequency, they are also finding that the preventable pollution was allowed by government agencies charged with protecting the public.

The public's concern for the environment cuts across social demographics and political party lines. Although concerns may be expressed differently, they are widespread and heartfelt. They are expressed as concerns for public health, our natural resources, and quality of life. A healthy environment is now being recognized as an essential ingredient to a healthy sustainable economy.

As President, we can expect George W. Bush to bring the environmental policies he has championed in Texas to the rest of the nation. Although he enjoys great popularity and a massive war chest of campaign contributions, little is known outside of Texas about the substance of those policies. His relatively few campaign statements about the environment have been late in coming and too often lacking in details. This is no accident. What George W. Bush hopes to do is to rewrite history and hide a shadowy backroom style of governing that runs counter to what he says he believes in.

The environment may well be one of George W. Bush's "skeletons in the closet." Now is the time for us to take it out, dust it off, and examine it closely.

# Following the Money
## *And Dancing with Those That Brung Him*

Money should always be considered when assessing the conduct of our public officials. In politics, it is money that turns "candidates" into "office holders." The truth is, as we say in the South, politicians too often "dance with those that brung them." The actions of our public officials *are* influenced by the campaign contributions they receive. This is true of Democrats and Republicans alike. It is the reason we have some of the best politicians that money can buy. Barring major campaign finance reform, this will not change.

While both major political parties talk about getting the influence of money out of politics, neither has made a serious effort to do so. Meanwhile, average citizens who cannot "ante up" with the big boys are finding it impossible to compete with the moneyed interests who routinely buy access and influence in the nation's capitol and houses of state government.

## The "For Sale" Sign at the Texas Statehouse

Texas is one of only 14 states in the country that place absolutely no limit on what wealthy donors can give a candidate.[1] Because of weak campaign laws, the sky is the limit for big money contributors in Texas, and they have reached for the sky with record high contributions to Texas politicians—especially George W. Bush. Although corporations are prohibited from making contributions directly to candidates, their Political Action Committees contribute without limitation, as do individuals, lobbyists and law firms associated with corporations.

Weak campaign laws give special interests the upper hand in Texas elections. "Because there are no limits, big donors get all the representation they can afford while the little guy gets left out," according to Texans for Public Justice whose research found that half the money in the last state election cycle came from donors who gave $25,000 or more.[2]

In an ideal world, campaign contributions would flow from like-minded supporters after hearing a candidate's message. High levels of contributions would reflect strong public support for the candidate's positions. Instead, campaigns are jumpstarted with massive contributions, often raised before the candidates have even articulated their positions on many key issues. Contrary to what the candidates would have us believe, this money is rarely given because of their charming personalities or compelling campaign rhetoric. Large contributions by special interest groups and people tied to those groups, are no more than investments. The return on those investments comes in the form of coveted access and influence over the elected official's decisions.

In many ways George W. Bush is no different than any other aspiring politician. He has needed large amounts of money to get where he is—and even more to get where he now wants to go. The challenge for those who want to examine Bush's record is to determine what access and influence has been bought with the large campaign contributions he has received.

Texas lawmakers have long understood that financial contributions can influence decisions and corrupt the political process. That is why Texas ethics law specifically prohibits a sitting governor from accepting campaign contributions during a legislative session.[3] However, this is precisely what Governor Bush did during the 1999 session. As this book reveals, he accepted hundreds of thousands of dollars from polluting industries that had a direct interest in legislation then under consideration.

The money of corporate polluters helped to jump-start Governor Bush's presidential campaign and his legislation saved them millions of dollars in the cost of pollution controls.

How could this happen?  The answer is simple, George W. Bush got around the prohibition because the money was given, not in support of his reelection campaign for governor, but *as support for his bid for the presidency.*  While this may be a legal distinction, excusing him from prosecution under state law, the moral violation should be clear.  He took money from special interests groups, allowed them to shape the legislation in meetings (sometimes closed to the public) and then he supported the legislation they wanted.

Did Governor Bush do anything that others haven't done?  Maybe not.  But, we may want to ask ourselves if this is how we want our government to be run.  Isn't this but another example of a politician sliding by on a technicality and ducking *personal responsibility*?  It is, therefore, no wonder that public interest organizations fear that campaign contributions have influenced Bush's support for polluter-friendly legislation.  When votes are on the table directly alongside campaign contributions, one can never be certain whether justice or cash made the final call.

National and state environmental groups charge that campaign contributions *have* influenced Bush's support for polluter friendly legislation.  Conversely, Governor Bush asks the public to ignore the massive contributions and believe that all of his decisions were based solely on "what was right for the people of Texas."[4] This is a leap of faith even the Texas legislature did not expect citizens to make.  Ethics laws exist because money *can* and too often *does* influence the decisions of our elected officials.  Numerous scandals, including "Watergate," "Iran-Contra" and sex have opened our eyes to the moral frailty of our government officials.  None deserve our blind faith and none are above reproach simply because they have a distinguished pedigree and a winning smile. Far too many have proven themselves unworthy of the trust that the American people have placed in them.

## Show Me the Money

In his 1994 and 1998 campaigns for Governor, George W. Bush received $1.5 million dollars from Texas companies who opposed strengthening air pollution legislation.[5] These same big business polluters gave more than $316,000 in the first 28 days of fundraising for his presidential campaign.[6]

Without question, large contributions are given by those who wanting something. Candidates can be judged by who's giving them money. It makes since to consider who's giving the money—and who's asking for it. That's exactly what an organization called Texans for Public Justice did. They found that an elite group of 212 individuals that George W. Bush's calls his "Pioneers" have delivered at least 24% of the *$90 million* raised for his presidential campaign.[7]

Who are these people that can raise so much money? The study released by Texans for Public Justice reveals they are corporate executives and special interest lobbyists, including a host of corporate polluters and others who seek special favors for their particular industries. With their help, Bush has raised more money than any other candidate in history.

## Hiding the Money

So, how then are voters to know when their public official's are being bought? One sure warning sign is their reluctant to disclose the money they receive. Why else would they not want the public to know who gives them money and how much. Politicians use many tricks when it comes to taking and reporting campaign contributions.

George W. Bush used one of the oldest. When he ran for re-election in 1998, he first filed his campaign contribution records only on paper, sometimes listing only two contributions per page. Although contributions of $50 and up had to be itemized, candidate Bush chose to list contributions of as little as a dollar. This created thousands of pages of unnecessary paper, hiding large contributions among the small.[8]

As a result, one filing contained 30,000 pages that had to be wheeled in to reviewers in boxes. This created an almost impossible task for those seeking to track Bush's big money contributions. After being criticized in several major newspaper articles, Governor Bush reversed himself and submitted the information electronically.[9]

The Bush Pioneers are believed to have delivered much more than $100,000 each. But presidential candidate Bush refuses to make this information public—even though his campaign tracks the amount of money raised by each Pioneer and even by each industry. The only Pioneers that the campaign has outed are those whom the campaign says already have delivered the requisite minimum of $100,000 apiece. Back in July 1999, Pioneer coordinator Jim Francis said that almost 400 individuals had taken the Pioneer pledge. Although Bush says disclosure is the cure to campaign finance problems, he will not say how many individuals are being tracked and how much each Pioneer has bundled for his campaign.[10]

## The Best Politicians that Money Can Buy?

One sure way to determine if an elected official has been improperly influenced with campaign cash is to determine if the contributor gained greater access and influence over the elected official. Was it greater than that received by others who had equally legitimate interests, but far less cash? Who benefited most from the elected official's decisions, and was the public's interest served?

The disturbing truth is that those who contribute the most too often reap the biggest benefits—and usually to the detriment of others.

We may not know for a fact that all of Bush's big dollar presidential campaign contributors will gain his favor. However, we can see how those who gave to his campaigns for Governor fared. How they fared in Texas tells us how they are likely to fare under a Bush Presidency.

This book assesses the environmental record of Texas Governor George W. Bush and how his decisions have affect people's lives. It also follows the money and the influence of some of his major campaign contributors. More than that, it reveals how he shapes and implements public policy. It tells us how he governs.

# George W. Bush's Environmental Legacy
## *A Skeleton in the Closet*

There are two things on which most everyone will agree: First, Texas, like other parts of the nation, has serious environmental problems. Second, to some extent, those problems existed even *before* George W. Bush became Governor.

Although former President George Bush declared himself "the environmental president," his son George W. Bush has not emphasized environmental issues since he became governor of Texas in 1995. This is true even though Texas' environmental problems rank among the worst in the nation. During his presidential campaign Bush has been criticized for avoiding issues pertaining to the environment. When he did speak up, he was criticized as doing so only in response to attacks from his rival candidates.

While his critics claim that Bush is hostile to environmental issues, his supporters claim his actions simply reflect the conservative politics of his home state. Even democratic lawmakers in Texas will sometimes be quick to defend Governor Bush's environmental record, blaming the lack of environmental progress on a "disinterested public."

The truth is Texans are far from being disinterested. In fact, over the last fifteen years Texas, like much of the nation, has witnessed a tremendous surge of popular support for environmental preservation and cleanup. Every single environmental issue that is addressed in this book has been advanced through the determination of grassroots citizen groups who have championed their particular cause to government officials, loudly demanding attention, then action.

Hundreds of "grassroots" environmental action groups have sprung up in urban and rural areas across the state. According to a 1991 *Dallas Morning* News article, "The movement cuts across political, social and racial lines. Its members seem united by only one thing: they are furious about pollution in their neighborhoods, as any public official who ever faced an angry community meeting can attest."

Unlike more well known 'mainstream' environmental groups with paid staffs and a broad focus on protecting natural resources, "grassroots" groups are made up of average citizens, passionately fighting to protect their own homes and families from nearby industrial polluters and leaking toxic waste sites. Their strongest members are usually women homemakers who volunteer their services. They are Republicans as often as they are Democrats. They are informed and determined—and they don't discriminate when it comes to holding public officials accountable.

Contrary to what the politicians say, people *do* care about the environment and they continue to put environmental issues in the news and at the center of public policy debates. Voters have turned local governments upside-down over issues such as whether or not a landfill, chemical plant or hazardous waste disposal facility should be located near a community—or built at all.

Large protests have taken place at the Texas Capitol over the years—some aimed directly at Governor Bush and his appointees. In February, March, April and May of 1999, when Bush was deciding to run for President, environmental protesters were arrested and jailed for peacefully marching on the public sidewalk in front of the Governor's mansion. Those arrested included a PTA mother and several refinery workers speaking out against air pollution at the plant where they worked.

A group called "Republican women unhappy with Governor Bush's environmental record" held an April 2000 news conference at the State Capitol to protest a controversial chemical plant approved by Bush's appointees. The group wanted a moratorium on new polluting industries in Harris County, which already has the dirtiest air in the nation.[11]

In June of 2000, people representing fifty different environmental organizations throughout the state demonstrated at the State Capitol before testifying at a legislative hearing on the state environmental agency. Their testimony, lasting into the night, was fueled by outrage at Governor Bush and his agency appointees over repeated favoritism for polluters at the public's expense.

When Texas politicians claim there is limited support for the environment in Texas, they are dead wrong. They are usually making excuses for their own unwillingness to stand up to business interests who have heavily contributed to Texas' pollution problems—and to their own campaigns. These powerful oil and gas companies, chemical companies, and utility companies, can exert tremendous political pressure on lawmakers. Most give money to Democratic and Republican politicians alike. By working both sides of the fence, but only one side of an issue, they make sure their hook is in place regardless of which side is in power.

Environmental organizations can't compete on an equal playing field with polluting industries. The power of organized citizens has rarely matched the power of organized money. When Texas environmental agencies were consolidated in 1991 under Governor Ann Richards, the word "environmental" was left out of the new agency's name. It was thought to be too "controversial."[12] That small but significant decision speaks volumes about the reluctance of Texas lawmakers and agency officials to challenge powerful business interests. That reluctance is no less evident today.

# Judging the Record
## *And Taking Personal Responsibility*

George W. Bush talks a lot about the need for people to take personal responsibility. He is one of the first to point out that we must each accept responsibility for the consequences of our actions. Time and again he has held rigidly to that philosophy, even when it has demanded that law-breakers pay the ultimate price. Having served as Governor of Texas for the last five years, George W. Bush needs accept at least some of that responsibility for Texas' continuing environmental problems. He needs to own up to the bad environmental policy decisions which he and his appointees have made. While he hasn't directly made all of those decisions, he appointed many of the people who did. Even public officials, whom he didn't appoint, made decisions that were undoubtedly influenced by the power of the Governor's office.

Governors, like Presidents, ask for and are given tremendous power. It is exercised when they overtly take action, or when they sit quietly by, giving only a wink and a nod. They exercise power even when they fail to act because the failure to take action also has consequences.

An elected official who claims to be a strong leader cannot, at the same time, deny his influence over others. Even when elected officials try to hide behind the decisions of their appointees, the public understands who is ultimately responsible. The acts of the powerful state environmental agency, the Texas Natural Resource Conservation Commission (TNRCC) are determined by the majority vote of its three commissioners—all of those commissioners are appointed by the Governor. Under Democratic and Republican administrations, their decisions have reflected the Governor's wishes.

## Statistics Don't Lie, But Liars Use Statistics

Over his five years as Governor, George W. Bush has certainly established enough of an environmental track record for others to judge. *Time* magazine, among others, has not judged it favorably. When *Time* issued a report card, Bush's pollution record received a grade of "D." According to *Time*, "Bush let industry write an anti-pollution measure, and believes voluntary plans, not regulation, can clean up the air and water. No wonder Texas has a world-class pollution problem."[13]

Governor Bush's critics point to pollution statistics showing Texas with some of the nation's most severe pollution problems—problems which they say have been made worse by Governor Bush. While Texans brag about being the first and biggest in many things, they are not so proud when it comes to those pollution statistics showing Texas "first" in pollution or as having some of the nation's "biggest" environmental problems.

Governor Bush tries to shift the responsibility by saying that he inherited many of these problems from his predecessor or that the state's high ranking in pollution statistics is only to be expected given the large concentration of gas, oil, and chemical industries which are important to the state's economy. Governor Bush and his campaign supporters are then quick to point to his environmental "accomplishments." However, little of this rhetoric withstands close scrutiny.

Tracking the rise and fall of pollution levels over the years can be tricky and misleading. Monitoring methods and reporting requirements have sometimes changed. This makes it harder to measure actual reductions and easier for those whose aim it is to distort the facts. To further confuse things, reported pollution levels are often estimates, calculated by those who are responsible for the pollution.[14]

Few politicians are willing to admit that a problem existing under their "watch" hasn't been solved or didn't, at the very least, improve significantly. Continued bad news does not usually advance political careers. However, at some point, even the Governor must admit to the truth. Despite the ever mounting evidence to the contrary, George W. Bush has not merely refused to take any responsibility for the failures of his administration in this area, but he has even gone so far as to boast that air quality in Texas has *improved* since he became Governor.

It is true that the levels of certain toxic chemicals, like benzene, ammonia, and chlorine, which are linked to cancer as well as to numerous neurological and developmental problems, have declined in Texas since the late 1980's. However, these reductions are attributed to the tightening of federal regulations governing hazardous air pollutants, more so than to the actions of any Texas Governor. It is also true, as Bush's aide point out, that Texas leads the nation in the reduction of toxic pollutants. However, the rates of reduction were higher under the previous Governor and the rates have declined since Bush took office, according to Texas environmental groups.[15].

Governor Bush also takes partial credit for the fact that Texas' national ranking in total toxic releases to the environment dropped from first for the years 1994 through 1997, to fifth in the nation for the year 1998. However, Texas would have remained first if the newly reporting industries, which included electric utilities and mines, had not been added to the statistics under the 1998 reporting requirements. Even before adding toxic releases from the new industries, toxic releases to the air and water in Texas actually *increased* from 1997 to 1998.[16]

It has been said that 'statistics don't lie, but liars use statistics.' Pollution statistics can be confusing, but when viewed objectively can also be a good indicator of the effectiveness of environmental policies.

When statistics are twisted and misused in political campaigns, they say much more about the politician using them than they do about the environment. The following are some of the more telling claims of Governor George W. Bush:

*"The air (in Texas) is cleaner since I became governor."*[17]
*--George W. Bush*

According to the EPA, eight-hour ozone violations for the state's top eight urban areas jumped 34 percent during the first four years of the Bush Administration.[18] In 1999 Texas registered the 24 worst smog readings in the country, including a reading in Houston that was twice the maximum level allowed by national health standards.[19] Houston also surpassed Los Angeles as the country's smoggiest city in 1999. Millions of Texans breath air not meeting federal minimum standards. All major metropolitan areas in the state are currently or will soon be in "non-attainment" status, as defined by the Environmental Protection Agency—meaning they must take steps to clean up their unhealthy air or face federal sanctions.[20] Industrial toxic air pollution rose from 108 million pounds in 1997 to approximately 110 million pounds in 1998, which is the most in the nation, making it No. 1 in the country.[21]

*Under legislation signed by Governor Bush, Texas became the 3rd state in the nation to require mandatory pollution reductions from power plants.*
*--Bush Presidential Campaign Web site*

George W. Bush did not support requiring "mandatory" pollution reductions from power plants until he signed the utility regulation bill at the very end of the legislative session. Until then, Bush steadfastly supported a "voluntary" pollution reduction program for power plants, just as he did for chemical plants and refineries. [22] Bush acted only after the EPA threatened to cut off federal highway funds because of his environmental agency's failure to draft a pollution plan for Dallas. That prospect prompted the powerful Texas highway-building lobby and Dallas financial and political establishment, to push for quick anti-pollution action. [23]

*Under two pieces of legislation supported and signed by Governor Bush, Texas will reduce their (industry's) emissions by more than 250,000 tons each year -- the equivalent of removing 5.5 million cars from Texas roads.*
*--Bush Presidential Campaign Web site*

There is little evidence to suggest this amount of pollution "will" be reduced. The first piece of legislation *required* pollution cuts from *power plants* and *is* expected to achieve significant reductions. However, Bush wanted the pollution cuts to be voluntary and did not support the legislative provisions *requiring* pollution cuts in power plants until late in the session, when it was likely to be passed anyway.

The rest of the pollution reductions are supposed to come as the result of a second piece of legislation establishing a *'voluntary'* program for *chemical plants and refineries*. Critics say the vast majority of these 800 plus facilities would not be persuaded to reduce pollution through a voluntary program. [24] The largest air polluter in Texas (over 100,000 tons annually), whose law firm was also Bush's largest campaign contributor, was not covered by key provisions of the legislation. [25]

Governor Bush's predictions are suspect because companies have not come forward to participate in his voluntary program at the rates he has predicted in the past. In March of 1998, Governor Bush announced that 36 companies joined his voluntary program and promised to cut 25,000 tons (out of the 900,000 tons) of grandfathered air pollution. However, *"Too Little-Too Late,"* a study released in November of 1998 by the Environmental Defense Fund, revealed that companies would only cut their emissions by one-sixth of what Governor Bush had promised—*if* the promises were actually fulfilled. As of November 1998 only three companies had actually reduced emissions, and then by only one-sixth of the promised total. Nine other companies acknowledged that they would receive permits under the "voluntary" program without actually reducing emissions to any significant degree.[26]

*From 1997 to 1998, while manufacturing activity in Texas increased by 25 percent over the last decade, Texas led the nation in reducing releases and disposal of toxics by 44 percent.*
*--Bush Presidential Campaign Web site*

From 1997 to 1998 toxic emissions to the air increased, as did toxic releases to surface waters. Texas fell from first place in overall toxic releases only because new categories of industries were added to the list of those required to report in 1998. Still, Texas' toxic releases were over 300 million pounds in 1998—up from 261 million pounds in 1997.[27] Toxic air pollution increased from 108 million pounds in 1997 to 110 million pounds in 1998. Counting the new industries toxic air pollution jumped to 288 million pounds. Toxic chemicals to the water also increased from 21.3 million pounds in 1997 to 25.1 million pounds.[28] While reductions in toxic emissions have occurred across most of the nation since 1995, 23 states have had larger reductions than Texas in this same period.[29]

*In 1997 Texans approved $60 million in bonds to restore state parks, and Governor Bush and the Texas Legislature provided $10 million more in 1999.*
*--Bush Pres. Campaign Web site*

The 1997 and 1999 allocations were emergency funding measures. There is nothing to indicate that Governor Bush advocated for this funding. Under Bush's administration, the state parks continue to suffer from a huge maintenance backlog of tens of millions of dollars. Governor Bush had the opportunity in the 1999 state legislative session, to increase funding for the state park system by supporting legislation to lift the cap on the dedication of revenue for state parks from the sporting goods sales tax. Bush failed to support this legislation. While George W. Bush has been governor, state purchases of new parkland has come to a virtual halt.[30]

Governor Bush, like democratic officeholders before him, claims his environmental critics are motivated by partisan politics. This is a charge that is transparently convenient but, not totally without merit. Some mainstream environmental groups have been reluctant to criticize Democrats for the same transgressions as their Republican counterparts. However, that bias does not necessarily lessen the truth of what they say. Criticism motivated by partisan politics can have merit, whether aimed at Democrats or Republicans.

While some of Texas' rankings on environmental concerns may be explained by the sheer amount of industrial facilities in the state, this is not always the case. Some rankings speak to the level of commitment Texas political leaders have towards environmental protection.

- Texas refineries are "Number 1" (the dirtiest) in the nation according to a state-by-state ranking which measures pollution per barrel of oil processed.[31]

- Texas is "Number 1" in Title VI civil rights complaints against the state environmental agency.[32]

- Texas is "Number 1" in the nation for the emission of greenhouse gasses. Texas has 7 percent of the nation' population, but it leads the nation in greenhouse gas emissions and accounts for 14 percent of the annual U.S. total. Texas is only one of 15 states that did not monitor global warming emissions or have a plan to reduce them.[33]

- Texas is 48th in the nation for spending on parks and recreation[34] and 46th for spending on the environment.[35]

The general concerns of Texas public interest environmental organizations are reflected in statements made by Public Employees for Environmental Responsibility, an alliance of state and federal employees working in pollution control, land management and wildlife protection agencies.

"Governor Bush's real approach for governing Texas has been to, 'Let Texas Industry run Texas.' His policies have consistently catered to the interests of industrial moguls, big landowners, and large contributors. Industry consultants and board members of polluting companies have been appointed to run Texas key regulating agencies. As a result, state environmental regulators have become largely ineffective, with inadequate resources or direction to enforce even the regulations still on the books. When confronted with the option of enforcing regulations or bypassing them, he has consistently chosen the latter. Under Bush's watch, Texas has deregulated many aspects of its environmental policy, including those governing wastewater discharges, pesticides, air pollution and certain nuclear waste. Governor Bush has said, 'What Texans can dream, Texans can do.' Clearly, Governor Bush never dreamed of cleaning up Texas' environment."[36] Public Employees for Environmental Responsibility says it "fears for the nation's environmental well-being if Governor Bush's agenda rises to the federal government level."

# George W. Bush: Double-Speak
## *And Other Misrepresentations*
*"*

All those who hold or aspire to public office are expected to tell us the truth. Even though Americans are quick to forgive and forget the transgressions of our leaders, especially in times of economic prosperity, we want them to be straight with us. It's when politicians are caught deceiving us that they get into real trouble. The act of deception often becomes the most serious transgression. And, for politicians who lean toward the self-righteous and sanctimonious, the act of deceiving can be a real skeleton in the closet.

## "Property Rights" *for Some*

*—bring back together*

Governor Bush has rallied millions of supporters around the battle cry of "property rights" and "local control." However, he and his allies in the legislature have acted to strip away local control and the property rights of millions of citizens. The following are a few of the examples that are detailed in following chapters.

- The citizens of Sierra Blanca, Midlothian, Pasadena, and other communities mentioned in this book, *should* have "property rights." However, citizens cannot sue Texas government for recklessly granting permits to big business polluters whose toxic and foul smelling pollution trespasses onto their property and into their homes.

- The citizens of Sierra Blanca have been forced to live with hundreds of tons of odorous New York City sludge dumped near their homes *each day*.

- Citizens of Pasadena have had to live with sulfur dioxide pollution that drifts into their community from a refinery permitted to operate despite thousands of air pollution violations.

- Citizens in the Midlothian area have had to live with air pollution containing toxic chemicals from a cement plant allowed by Bush appointees, to burn hazardous waste as "fuel."

Governor Bush does *not* extend his concept of "property rights" to citizens whose property is damaged by big business polluters. Citizens, who lose the use and enjoyment of their property, and in some cases the value of their property, are not considered or given any right or recourse under Bush's "property rights" agenda. Neither can citizens sue the state agencies for taking taxpayers money and then failing to enforce the laws that are supposed to protect people and their property. In fact, Governor Bush's support for "tort reform" makes it harder for pollution victims to sue polluters for the harm they do.

## "Controlling the Locals"

Although Governor Bush claims to be a supporter of "local control" he has acted to strip local control from citizens and their local governments. At the same time Governor Bush's appointees to state agencies have failed to protect citizens, he has acted to take away the ability of local governments to protect citizens. Bush's appointees have granted permits to big business special interests over the objections of city and county governments.

- Citizens and their local governments were denied "local control" when Bush's appointees ignored their opposition and allowed the amount of New York City sewage sludge coming to Sierra Blanca in Hudspeth County to be *tripled*.

- Local control" was denied when Governor Bush lobbied to establish federal legislation that would make Texas the host -state for the nation's radioactive waste.

Bush lobbied to bring this waste to Texas over the objections of dozens of county and city governments in the southwest part of the state where the dump was proposed.  Governor Bush lobbied to make sure the source of the waste coming to Texas would not be limited to two states, but instead could come from any state in the nation.  Although Bush says he wants to "Let Texans Run Texas," the legislation he supported established a commission to over see the radioactive waste program that was to be appointed by the Governor—not elected by the people.  Furthermore, the state legislature would have no control over the commission's actions.

• *Bush didn't tell the truth* when he told news reporters and the people of El Paso in April of 1998, that the radioactive waste targeted for their area was mostly medical waste like X-rays.[37]  Four months earlier, Bush had written a letter urging that the State of Maine send its dismantled nuclear power plant waste to Texas—even its oversized radioactive components.[38]

• Governor Bush signed legislation into law that was found to be unconstitutional by the Texas Supreme Court because it gave powers that rightfully belong to the public—to private corporations.[39]  The legislation was pushed by developers and removed 8,000 acres from the City of Austin's jurisdiction and environmental regulation.[40]  The area in question had, after 20 years of debate, come under strong water quality protections through the "Save Our Springs" citizen initiative.  With Bush's signature, the legislation prohibited the City's enforcement of land use ordinances, pollution control programs, water quality ordinances, subdivision requirements and more.  Not only did the legislation remove environmental protections, but it also removed the real estate from consideration for annexation for 20 years.  This was a heavy financial blow to a city that had spent millions on building the infrastructure in the area.

• Governor Bush did not sign, but allowed another piece of developer-backed legislation to become law. It took "local control" from citizens in Travis County by designating a so-called "water quality district."[41] The land within the district was removed from the jurisdiction of local governments. They could no longer regulate the use of parkland or adopt rules protecting the watershed or endangered species. The legislation established a new governmental entity that usurped local control. This nine-member commission was appointed by Governor Bush and not elected by local citizens. It prohibited creation of local governments or political subdivisions—even if approved by all the landowners—unless the hand picked commissioners for the district approved. This law was also ruled to be unconstitutional by a Texas district court and the Texas State Court of Appeals.[42]

# Bush's "New" Approach
## *The Same Dance to a Different Tune*

In truth, there is nothing new about George W. Bush's approach to the environment.  It's an approach one would expect from someone with roots in the oil and gas industry.  It is also no different than the approach that the industry itself has advocated for years.  Governor Bush's legislative initiatives during his term in office mirror industry's wish list for environmental policies.  Common goals are to:

- Limit liability for polluters,
- Reduce public input on regulatory decisions,
- Allow 'voluntary' instead of mandatory compliance with  environmental laws
- Allow polluters to design their own 'flexible' anti-pollution programs.

*"This country is entering a new era of environmental policy.   An  era  of  cooperation,  not  coercion,  of responsibility, not heavy-handed regulation."*
*--George W. Bush*

Bush's statement speaks for itself.  He considers environmental regulation to be "coercion" and "heavy-handed."  He doesn't see regulations or legal actions as necessary ways to solve problems.  According to Bush's campaign, he stresses a "cooperative" approach with business and industrial leaders emphasizing "voluntary" programs instead of "regulatory mandates" to solve problems. To the extent that he admits that regulations are necessary, he emphasizes that they must be "flexible." [43]

Bush's views on the environment are a dream come true for industrial polluters that have long resented regulation and resisted being held accountable in the courts.   It is understandable that they have pumped millions of dollars into his election campaigns.

The "cooperative approach" championed by Governor Bush is music to the ears of corporate polluters. Through campaign contributions, they are assured of more than their share of seats when it comes time to partner-up at the negotiating table and "cooperate." As his record makes clear, his idea of a "cooperative approach" and a so-called "partnership" means cooperation with industry. To Bush, these terms do not involve any meaningful public participation by non-business interests.

George W. Bush says he wants to limit government's role, especially that of the federal government, in setting priorities for environmental cleanup. His slogan, "Let Texans Run Texas" makes this clear. However, as Governor Bush's record also makes clear, he does not object to government fiats and regulations that strip control from local communities and offer protections and benefits to big business polluters. He even supports federal environmental legislation that strips control from local and state governments, so long as benefits, and no way hampers, big business special interests. When the nuclear power industry needed more places to dump their radioactive waste, Bush supported federal legislation to make sure it would come to Texas.

Governor Bush's positions on the environment reflect that he holds a double standard when it comes to applying and enforcing the law. One standard allows "flexibility" and "voluntary" compliance for big business (and his major campaign contributors). His other standard is one he applies to the general public: it calls for strict interpretation and swift, certain, and unwavering enforcement of the law. Individual citizens are required to recognize that there are "consequences" when they don't exercise "personal responsibility." Bush's philosophy of "flexibility" and "voluntary compliance" for corporate polluters allows them to avoid their personal and social responsibility. The "flexibility" he wants to see in laws and regulations provides industry with the "wiggle room" needed to delay or altogether avoid complying with laws and standards.

Another area of Governor Bush's double standard, or "double speak" concerns his requirement for government's use of the "best science" in making environmental decisions.[44] This familiar industry buzzword has been frequently used to argue against the need for strict environmental standards. What has been made clear over the years is that science is often for sale. The definition of "best science" can be influenced by business concerns with unlimited resources to pay scientists to reach needed conclusions.

If the "best science" has yet to prove, beyond a doubt, that an environmental or public health risk exists, this absence of proof is too often used as an excuse *not* to take action. This is too often the case, even when common sense and mounting evidence says it is better to act and err on the side of caution. The absence of absolute proof of harm does not itself prove that harm does not or will not occur. As many pollution victims have learned, by the time the "best science" proves beyond a doubt that something is harmful, the damage has been done and all that remains is to tally the numbers of victims.

In short, George W. Bush's approach to environmental protection is the approach that has, for years, been advocated by those who are responsible for much of the pollution. A *Washington Post* interview with a chemical company executive summed up industry's feelings about Bush,

> "'We like Bush because of his evenhandedness, his grasp of our issues,' said an executive in the chemical industry, which has more plants in Texas than in any other state. 'We see him as someone we can work with' on the environment. 'We want to do things voluntarily,' as Bush prefers, he said 'rather than by command and control out of Washington.'"[45]

There is no doubt that the oil, gas and chemical industry wants to make sure that George W. Bush is elected into the highest and most powerful office possible and that he remains there for a long time. They have invested and will continue to invest what some say are obscene amounts of money in his various campaigns to make sure this dream becomes a reality. In his 1994 and 1998 campaigns for Governor, George W. Bush received $1.5 million dollars from Texas companies who did not want to be forced into reducing their pollution air pollution levels.[46] When he began raising money for his Presidential run, grandfathered polluters stepped up to the plate with more than $316,000 in the first 28 days of fundraising.[47] They gave to Bush because they knew he would give in return.

## Too Much Carrot and Not Enough Stick

George W. Bush's approach to environmental protection won't work for the nation for the same reasons it hasn't worked for the people of Texas. It is an approach that makes it profitable to pollute.

The evidence of greed and profiteering at the public's expense can be seen throughout all of the nation's environmental problems. There are thousands of abandoned toxic waste sites where, instead of spending money on pollution prevention and safer disposal, companies simply dumped wastes into leaking pits before pocketing their profits and moving on down the road. The discharging of waste into the nation's waterways have rendered many of them unsuitable as drinking water supplies or for recreation. Major metropolitan areas are choking from air pollution made worse by industries that maximize short-term profits by refusing to invest in the best available pollution controls.

Environmental laws, like the Clean Water Act, Clean Air Act, and the Resource Conservation and

Recovery Act, were passed to stop the poisoning of people
and the environment.    Much of this environmental
destruction took place when industrial concerns enjoyed
what was in effect a 'voluntary' program allowing them to
prevent pollution as they saw fit.

The same environmental laws and regulations
which Governor Bush considers to be "coercive" and
"heavy-handed," have helped to protect the nation's
environment, and in some cases, help clean it up.  Since
1970 when the Clean Air Act went into effect, the
nationwide emissions of the six major air pollutants
dropped 29 percent.    In this same time period, the
country's population grew 28 percent and the gross
domestic product doubled.[48]

The enactment and administration of these laws at
the national level, which some call "command and control
out of Washington DC", ensures that the same standards
exist across the nation and boundaries of commerce.  Far
from being what George W. Bush calls "heavy-handed"
with local communities, federal environmental laws assure
that each citizen at the local level is guaranteed the same
clean air and water as citizens in every other state.  When
state and federal governments fail to protect citizens, these
so-called "heavy-handed" laws ensure that each citizen
has the right to use the courts to protect their homes and
families.

A case in point is demonstrated in Texas, where
Exxon's massive Baytown industrial complex was
discharging billions of gallons of untreated wastewater
into the waters of Galveston Bay.  Because Exxon chose not
to invest in an adequate treatment system, heavy rains
routinely caused Exxon's under-sized treatment system to
overflow and carry oily wastes into Galveston Bay.  The
Coast Guard fined Exxon for some discharges it found bad
enough to classify as oil spills.  Even the local government
in Harris County urged that these discharges permitted by
the state agency be stopped.  Unfortunately, Governor

Bush's appointees, who evidently did *not* believe in "local control" when it came to stopping Exxon's pollution, bowed to Exxon.

When the state environmental agency, run by Bush's appointees, refused to stop Exxon's discharges, citizens used their rights as guaranteed by the federal Clean Water Act and filed a lawsuit against the company in federal court. It was only after Exxon was made to stop the illegal discharges and pay the citizens' legal expenses that the company finally invested the money to enlarge its treatment system.[49]

The Exxon case not only demonstrates the need for the federal regulations and legal actions that Bush opposes, it demonstrates why Bush's concept of "voluntary compliance" won't work. Exxon could have voluntarily invested in upgrading its treatment system to stop its oily discharges at any time. Instead, it chose to delay expenditures and maximize profits at the public's expense—until it was forced by citizens and the federal government to do otherwise.

The failure of George W. Bush's "voluntary" approach to environmental protection is also illustrated in Texas where it was tried with old, outdated industrial facilities for almost 30 years. When the Texas Clean Air Act was passed in 1971, existing power plants, refineries and chemical plants, were "grandfathered" and exempted from the law. Facilities built later were covered by the law and required to have better pollution controls. In 1971 these "grandfathered" polluters said that over time, they would voluntarily comply with the law, to the same standards imposed on newer facilities. Instead, most continued business as usual. By 1998 these industrial facilities, some of the oldest, biggest, and dirtiest in Texas, were responsible for 36% of the state's industrial air pollution, or over 900,000 tons.[50] They emit as much ozone pollution-causing chemicals as 18 million automobiles.[51]

Everyone in business does not act irresponsibly. However, even those who chose to invest in pollution prevention can find themselves at an economic disadvantage when their direct competitors refuse to make similar investments. As long as some are allowed to save money by polluting, others will have the financial incentive, if not the necessity, to do the same.

Governor W. Bush says he believes in "market-driven solutions" to environmental problems. In fact, many of our environmental problems exist because polluters have wanted to better position themselves in the "market." To Bush, a market driven solution is limited to situations where government creates an economic incentive, often at a direct expense to the taxpaying public, just to do what is morally and legally right.

Governor Bush and his industry supporters refuse to recognize the value of "disincentives" to pollute as a "market-driven solution." When the worst polluters are made to pay increased fees or significant penalties for their pollution, they, in turn, lose profits. Their position in the "market" suffers as a direct result of non-compliance. This places competitors who act responsibly in a better market position. This economic disincentive to pollute acts as an incentive for the worst polluters to act more responsibly.

Moving some industrial polluters from outdated, environmentally harmful business practices to new environmentally conscious operations can be likened to moving a stubborn mule that is comfortable where he stands. Sometimes it takes a carrot and a stick to get the mule to move. Bush's approach to encouraging environmental protection is not to use a carrot and a stick. It's all carrot and no stick. This can create gluttonous, lazy asses that obstinately refuse to change.

History has proven that strong laws and enforcement are essential to protecting the environment and the public health. If we weaken or fail to enforce these laws, we will be ignoring the lessons of the past and turning back the clock of progress.

Industries that cause environmental problems can also provide products and much needed products and jobs. While industry representatives may be "stakeholders" with the right to participate in environmental decision making, they should not be granted disproportionate, special access or undue influence with public officials who have the duty to represent all of the citizenry. The kind of environmental "partnership" that George W. Bush has practiced in Texas is a partnership between government and special interests with little or no inclusion of the general public, especially those who have the most at stake. The citizens who are the victims of pollution are the voices and concerns invariably excluded from George W. Bush's "partnerships" concerning matters affecting the environment.

# Saying No to Clean Air
## *Breaking the Promise of the Clean Air Act*

As knowledge about air pollution and its accompanying health effects advances, it is clear that much of the nation still faces major problems. Whether or not the air we breathe is getting cleaner is often debated and never resolved. Polluters, often armed with cold hard statistics, argue that enough has been done and additional clean-up will simply cost too much money.

As the American Lung Association points out, people grid-locked in heavy traffic or living downwind of refineries, papermills, power plants or incinerators "know in their hearts that the air isn't clean enough, and that their children and parents are at risk."[52] Cold, hard statistics, including a rising body count and increased health care costs, support the view that more still needs to be done.

Texas has a long history of broken promises and failure when it comes to complying with the federal Clean Air Act. It has been forty-five years, beginning in 1955, since the United States adopted national legislation designed to keep our air clean. The amended federal Clean Air Act of 1970 required acceptable pollution levels, or standards, to be established by the EPA for six common air pollutants. These pollutants are, particulate matter, carbon monoxide, sulfur dioxide, oxides of nitrogen and lead. The standards set maximum levels that are acceptably safe for human health. The standards are based on scientific research and change as more is learned about their health effects.

When areas within a state have a problem meeting (or attaining,) these health-based standards, they are classified as "non-attainment" areas. The law says a state's environmental agency must prepare plans for these areas which are to be submitted, approved and implemented within certain deadlines. These "State Implementation Plans" detail how and when "non-attainment" areas will attain compliance with the law. Areas that do not comply with the law can face federal sanctions and lose federal highway funds. Taking away highway construction funds helps to limit traffic increases and associated air pollution.

While some politicians portray the federal Clean Air Act as 'heavy-handed' and 'intrusive,' most citizens know better. They know that dirty unhealthy air allowed in one area can cause otherwise clean air in another area to become dirty and unhealthy. As history makes clear, some local and state governments would never take the necessary steps to clean without federal mandates. This is especially true of states like Texas, where polluters that contribute to the pollution problem, also contribute heavily to elected officials. Uniform federal Clean Air Act standards that are enforced uniformly across the country are both fair and necessary to protect the nation's health. The right to breathe clean, healthy air belongs to all of us—not just to some.

## Delay and Denial

The approach of Texas government to cleaning up the air has been to do no more, and usually less, than required by the Environmental Protection Agencies. For decades Texas has submitted State Implementation Plans that have been inadequate and late in arriving. In the late 70's, the state agency asked that its deadline for a plan to control ozone in the Houston metropolitan area be extended to 1987. In 1983 the EPA threatened sanctions because Texas failed to submit a plan for a vehicle maintenance and inspection program in the Houston metropolitan area. Instead of applying sanctions, the EPA backed down and extended the deadline.

In 1984 Texas was notified that plans were needed to show how Dallas, Tarrant, and El Paso Counties would be able to comply with the Clean Air Act pollution standards.[53] Texas requested and received an extension of the deadline until mid-1985. By 1987 the EPA was again threatening sanctions because Texas failed to meet the deadline. In 1986, 1988 and 1990 the standards for sulfur dioxide were exceeded in the Houston area and were predicted to be exceeded in the future.[54] In the early 1990's "non-attainment areas" in violation of ozone standards were classified according to their severity. The Houston-Galveston area was classified as "severe," the Beaumont-Port Arthur and El Paso areas were "serious," and the Dallas area was "moderate."[55] By February of 1998, the Dallas-Fort Worth area "serious." Ozone is considered one of the most dangerous of the common air pollutants.

In May of 1999 the state failed to meet the deadline for an acceptable plan detailing how the Dallas-Fort Worth area would reduce ozone levels. Two months later, the EPA threatened to suspend federal highway money if a plan was not developed by the next year. The state environmental agency's latest plan for bringing the Dallas-Fort Worth area into compliance with health standards for ozone was not submitted until April of 2000. The plan for controlling ozone pollution in the eight county Houston –Galveston area, which is in "severe" violation, was not submitted until July of 2000. As of August 2000, both the Central Texas Austin/San Antonio area and the East Texas Longview-Tyler-Marshall areas were soon expected to fall into "non-attainment" of federal clean air standards.

The deadline for actually cleaning up the air to meet the health-based ozone standards in the state's two largest metropolitan areas of Houston–Galveston and Dallas–Fort Worth, has been extended to the year 2007. Many people doubt they will be breathing healthy air even by then. Because Texas politicians, including Governor Bush, have failed to address the problem, citizens are now facing more extreme, unpopular, and costly clean-up measures.

## 'First' with the 'Worst' for Ozone Pollution

In the five years since 1994, Texas has assumed the dubious status of having the highest levels of ozone of any state in the nation. Ozone is linked to lung damage and is a primary ingredient in smog. Since Governor Bush took office, Texas has recorded ozone levels surpassing even Los Angeles, Chicago, and New York City.[56] Air quality problems in Texas have reached what some consider "crisis" proportions, with every major urban area in non-attainment or near "non-attainment" status of federal air quality standards.

Ozone is the most widespread and dangerous of the common air pollutants. In the earth's upper atmosphere, ozone occurs naturally and protects us by shielding the sun's harmful rays. In the lower atmosphere, ozone develops when pollutants react chemically in the presence of sunlight. The American Lung Association, in their "State of the Air 2000" report, described the effect ozone has on our health;[57]:

> At levels routinely encountered in most American cities, ozone burns through cell walls in lungs and airways. Tissues redden and swell. Cellular fluid seeps into the lungs and over time their elasticity drops. Susceptibility to bacterial infections increases, probably because ciliated cells that normally expel foreign particles and organisms have been killed and replaced by thicker, stiffer, non-ciliated cells. Scars and lesions form in the airways. At ozone levels that prevail through much of the year in California and other warm-weather cities, healthy, non-smoking young men who exercise can't breathe normally. Breathing is rapid, shallow and painful...Children at summer camp lose the ability to breathe normally as ozone levels rise...

According to research by the American Lung Association, more than 132 million Americans live in areas where the air quality received a 'Failing' grade in their report. Among those living within counties that received a 'Failing' grade for their ozone levels, there are an estimated 16 million Americans over 65, over 7 million asthmatics, 29 million children under age 14, and 7 million adults with chronic bronchitis.

A 1996 study by the American Lung Association and Harvard School of Public Health linked increases in emergency room visits and hospitalizations for respiratory conditions to high ozone levels in thirteen cities.[58] In some areas, hospital visits doubled on high ozone days.

Asthma is an inflammatory disease of the bronchial tubes and affects more than 17 million Americans. It also results in more than 5,000 deaths each year. According to numerous studies, people with asthma have more attacks during ozone alerts, thereby requiring increased medication or, too often, even hospitalization. In addition to affecting those with asthma, ozone impacts people with other chronic lung diseases such as emphysema and bronchitis. It appears to also increase the risk of respiratory infections.[59]

While George W. Bush and his campaign staff claim the air has gotten "cleaner" over the last five years, millions of people living in major metropolitan areas now breathe air not meeting federal minimum standards. Texas registered 24 of the worst smog readings in the country for 1999, including a reading in Houston on Oct. 7, 1999 that was twice the maximum level allowed by national health standards.[60] The area's highest ozone reading in 1999—also the nation's highest—was 251 parts per billion (ppb).[61] The Houston area recorded *eight of the ten* highest ozone levels in the country for the year. Ozone levels begin to be unhealthy at 125 ppb under the one hour standard and 85 ppb under the eight-hour standard.[62]

In July of 2000, an ozone reading 206 parts per billion was taken in central Houston and triggered a "very unhealthy" alert. Ozone measurements classified as "unhealthy" were recorded at six other Houston-area sites a few days earlier. As of August 21, 2000 there have already been 23 days when ozone exceeded healthy levels.[63]

## More Delay and Denial

While other states have taken actions to combat air pollution, Texas and local officials have pushed back EPA compliance deadlines, requested waivers on cutting back ozone emissions, and delayed submitting air pollution clean-up plans. By 1995, when Governor Bush took office, the EPA was already exploring the need for new, stricter controls to address ozone pollution. Meanwhile, the Bush administration, together with polluting industries, attempted to circumvent the Clean Air Act regulations and obstruct enforcement of the law.

In May of 1995 Governor Bush appointed Ralph Marquez to the state environmental agency, Marquez was an executive with Monsanto Chemical Company for thirty years and active in the Texas Chemical Council. Within weeks a plan for smog advisories in the Houston area was scuttled. Public warnings of high ozone levels had been used for years in other smog ridden urban areas. Houston was the largest city in the country with a serious smog problem and no public awareness campaign. Although citizen groups and the regional air quality planning committee had agreed to issue public ozone warnings through local media, Houston business leaders were reluctant to publicize the city's dirty air problem. The state environmental agency, the TNRCC, crippled the project when it sided with business interests and simply refused to supply the necessary monitoring results for publication.[64]

## Bush's Plan to Lower the Ozone Standards

One way to make a problem *appear* to go away, is to stop calling it a problem. This is what the administration of George W. Bush attempted to do concerning ozone pollution. The appointment of his second TNRCC commissioner in August of 1995, was part of this effort. Bush announced his second appointee to the TNRCC, Barry McBee, in August of 1995. McBee was an attorney with the pro-industry lobby law firm Thompson & Knight. According to environmentalists, McBee, while working at the Texas Department of Agriculture, led efforts to roll back "Right-to-Know" laws on pesticide use that protected farmworkers.[65]

With a majority of Bush appointees on the board, the TNRCC began an aggressive effort to challenge and undermine proposed EPA air quality regulations that would strengthen ozone pollution standards.

In an effort to hide increasing air pollution levels that were being recorded in Texas, the TNRCC lobbied the EPA in August of 1995 to average the results of ozone monitors.[66] In October the TNRCC announced its own formal Texas Ozone position which worked at revising the national health standards for ozone. The TNRCC's plan was to use a statistical "averaging" scheme for the air pollution monitors that continually recorded ozone levels.

This number crunching would essentially average out most of the high ozone readings (that violated the standards in large urban areas) and even-out the severe pollution in the Houston-Galveston area and bring it into compliance with health standards. This "compliance" was not to be reached by reducing pollution, but by measuring it differently. Critics said the Texas Plan, which included other changes as well, represented an 'out of sight, out of mind' approach to air pollution problems.[67]

Bush's Pollution Plan Goes to Washington

From an overall economic perspective, the least expensive way to reduce ozone levels is to reduce emissions from industrial polluters, according to studies conducted by the EPA. The TNRCC's "Texas Plan" avoided the heart of the problem and instead, focussed on changing how the problem was reported. The plan was criticized by environmental and public health organizations as a blatant attempt to protect polluting industries that wanted to avoid spending additional money on pollution controls.

The state agency's efforts to protect industry profits hit new heights when, in early November of 1995, Bush appointee Ralph Marquez testified before the Subcommittees On Oversight And Investigations And Health And Environment, The House Committee On Commerce in Washington, DC. The congressional testimony of Commissioner Marquez epitomized the Bush administration's policy on controlling ozone. Marquez said, "EPA's use of ozone (smog) as a surrogate for control of other dangerous pollutants should be discontinued." Marquez went on to explain that this was because ozone was not hazardous. "After all, ozone is not a poison or a carcinogen. It is a relatively benign pollutant compared to other environmental risks," he testified.

In effect, Bush appointee Ralph Marquez questioned the reliability of accepted scientific methods commonly used across the nation. He went on to say, "The ozone standard should be revised as indicated by the Texas proposal It is time that we as a nation step out of the current ozone control philosophy box and reassess our air pollution priorities." The question presented here is whether the priorities held by the majority of living and breathing Americans, as well as the public health community, are the same priorities held by the man who wants to be President.

In this case, Bush's administration questioned the "best science" which established national air standards reflecting careful scientific and regulatory consideration. This contradicts Bush's campaign pledge to rely on the "best science" to set his environmental policies. Apparently, he doesn't intend to rely on the "best science" if it runs counter to the needs of big business polluters.

## Bush Appointees Oppose Ozone and Particulate Rules

When, in 1997, the EPA formally proposed strengthening the standards for ozone and fine particulates, Governor Bush's TNRCC appointees echoed industry's objections and opposed the new standards. The TNRCC, instead of focussing on public health and the environment, once again targeted its concerns on the financial cost of pollution reductions to industry. Bush appointee Barry McBee said, "It should not be too much to ask of government, especially given the potential effects on families, business and industry and the staggering costs of regulations, to adopt standards that are both clear and based on sound science."[68]

If the EPA standard was approved, the TNRCC's own calculations showed the number of areas out of compliance in Texas would increase to nine—more than any other state. This was the last thing Governor Bush and his appointees wanted to see. To allow higher levels of pollution without falling out of compliance, the TNRCC had to average ozone measurements over eight hours. TNRCC said this would protect public health and, "avoid the creation of new non-attainment areas within Texas."[69]

Governor Bush's TNRCC appointees also protested the EPA establishing a more protective standard for fine particulates. They objected under the guise that more information was needed on the effect of breathing small particles "on human health."[70]   Again, the Bush administration was willing to ignore the "best science" which established that the fine particles of soot were known to be dangerous.[71] These particles get into the deepest recesses of the lungs and are not readily removed by the body's natural cleaning process. These tiny particles are also known to carry other chemical pollutants deep into the lungs.

A May 1996 report by the Natural Resources Defense Council estimated that Texas power plants emit particulates that are responsible for 2,617 premature deaths of Texans each year.[72] More than a dozen scientific studies have shown pronounced changes in heart patterns in the elderly when levels of particulates increase in the air. Epidemiologists in 70 cities around the world have consistently found that more people are hospitalized and even die when particulate pollution rises even in a moderate amount.[73]

Why was the TNRCC's main concern the economic costs associated with additional pollution controls rather than the social and public health cost of ignoring the pollution from particulates and ozone? Bush appointee McBee attempted to justify the agency's position by stating, "The costs of air pollution controls designed to achieve the proposed standards would dwarf the marginal ozone benefits, while whatever benefits might come from the new particulate standards are too uncertain to compare with the huge costs.[74]

Are the costs "huge" compared to the benefits to public health? The EPA estimated that the stricter standards would cost $8 billion but, would prolong the lives of 20,000 Americans every year and save from $51 billion to $112 billion in health costs.[75]

The state agency's position reflects the real priorities of Governor Bush's appointees. By delaying the more protective standards, industry saves $8 billion while the lives of 20,000 Americans are shortened at an increase of $51 billion to $112 billion dollars in health care costs and reduced productivity from lost time at work.

The Bush administration's real policy decision is to decide who will pay. Either industry pays to reduce pollution, or citizens pay if pollution isn't reduced. Simple should make the morally correct answer clear, not to mention the 20,000 lives who would be affected. However, Bush's position appears to be based on *who* pays—not who pays the most. The public pays the tab, even though the cost to industry is much less.

To defend its opposition to the stronger (Clean Air Act) standards, the TNRCC claimed the number of days when ozone pollution was over the limits in Texas was actually *declining* over the years. The TNRCC stated, "A statewide decline in the number of ozone exceedance days each year since 1988 demonstrates that EPA's current ozone standards is working in Texas communities..." This statement, together with a series of supporting charts, was presented in the TNRCC's official publication.[76]

On the surface, the information appeared accurate. However, an analysis by the Environmental Defense Fund's Texas Office discredited TNRCC's information and determined that it was misleading and factually wrong. According to the Environmental Defense Fund, "There has *not* been a decline in the number of ozone exceedance days each year since 1988. Between 1988 and 1996 the number of exceedance days increased in 1990, 1994, and 1995 relative to the previous year."[77]

So, how was the state environmental agency able to mislead the public and conclude ozone pollution was getting better when it was actually getting worse? The Environmental Defense Fund singled out one of the TNRCC charts showing the number of days when ozone pollution was over the limits. By omitting the odd numbered years (including 1995 when there were 68 days when the ozone limits was exceeded), the TNRCC had also skewed the overall picture. The Environmental Defense Fund concluded that TNRCC's omission was intentional since other charts showing population growth and gross domestic product did not exclude these years.[78]

## The Cost of Delay

Before Bush was elected Governor, the previous administration had gone through the expensive process of gearing up for a vehicle inspection and maintenance program that had been designed to reduce automobile emissions for the most polluted areas of the state; Dallas-Fort Worth, Houston-Galveston, and Beaumont-Port Arthur. However, Mr. Bush agreed with the angry motorists and the talk-radio crowd who thought the program extreme and didn't think motorists should be inconvenienced. And, he sure didn't like Washington telling Texans what to do.

The first legislation Mr. Bush signed as governor, was a bill that put the emissions tests on hold. As many expected, the air in these areas got worse. His administration's refusal to address air pollution problems cost the public in more ways than one. In July of 1997, the TNRCC was ordered to pay a settlement of $140 million for breaking the contract with Tejas Testing, the company that had agreed to administer the vehicle emission program.[79] To comply with the court ordered settlement, Governor Bush and the Legislature chose to cut the TNRCC budget an additional $125 million - an 18% decrease. This forced another round of reductions in the agency's operations that included reduced enforcement, fewer field inspections, decreased planning, and monitoring of current cleanup strategies.[80]

When Governor Bush officially filed for Texas' presidential primary, he defended his environmental record by pointing to his recent call for automobile manufacturers to produce cleaner-burning vehicles and the Texas Natural Resource Conservation Commission to establish "tough automobile emission standards." When asked by a reporter if it had been a mistake for the Legislature to scuttle auto emissions testing in 1995 - his first year in office - and whether his new push for cleaner fuels and cleaner-burning vehicles was too little, too late, Bush said, *"No."*

"I'm not so sure your premise that the air would have been cleaner if we'd had centralized testing in the Metroplex or Harris County would have worked," Bush said. "I think that was an assumption that just wasn't valid. I believe our plan, or the plan that's now working its way through the process, will clean up the air in the big cities."[81]

In fact, the Houston area smog plan, finally proposed in July of 2000, calls for strict new tailpipe tests for cars and trucks, beginning in Harris County next year and later extending to the seven other counties. Because the air in the region has gotten so bad, other more extreme (and unpopular) measures are being proposed as well. These include banning the use of heavy construction equipment and the use of gasoline powered lawn equipment from 6:00a.m until noon. This will hurt the construction industry and the many commercial lawn care services. The plan also calls for lowering of speed limits to 55 mph.

Some say that the Houston metroplex, and possibly other areas of Texas, may not be able to meet EPA compliance deadlines—even with the "aggressive" cleanup program Governor Bush now brags about on the campaign trail.[82] The greatest fear of many environmentalists is that George W. Bush, if elected President, will move to weaken the Clean Air Act by lowering the standards or removing the threat of economic sanctions. They feel the threat of economic sanctions is the 'stick' that is necessary to move state and local governments to clean up the air. Withholding highway funds is the appropriate form of economic sanctions because it limits additional pollution by discouraging increased traffic levels.

What Governor Bush has created, either by design or circumstance, is the perfect situation for an opportunistic politician. Here's one likely scenario.

Governor Bush's failure to address air pollution problems gets him contributions from business interests that didn't want to spend money on pollution prevention. Because the pollution has gotten so bad, severe and unpopular measures are necessary to solve the problem. Instead of accepting responsibility for failing to do something about the problem earlier, George W. Bush directs the public's anger at the "regulations" and "federal mandates." Most citizens are primed for his message that says federal regulations are "heavy handed" and "coercive." After all, they are now facing driving and other restrictions. With the contributions from polluting business interests who jump-started his campaign, Governor Bush could win the election to the Presidency. Believing in "cooperation" and "partnerships" as he does, he will again partner up with his big business polluters to write a new environmental policy. That will stress the same "flexibility" and "voluntary" compliance that led to the problem in the first place.

*"This country is entering a new era of environmental policy. An era of cooperation, not coercion, of responsibility, not heavy-handed regulation."*
*--George W. Bush*

# The Moneymaker
*Keeping the Grandfather of Pollution Loopholes*

For nearly thirty years, air pollution has been a growing problem in Texas. When Governor Bush took office, the public was growing sick and tired of air pollution. With metropolitan areas facing economic sanctions for failing to meet federal Clean Air Act Standards, citizens were demanding that industrial polluters accept their share of the responsibility to clean up the air. A series of articles in major newspapers began to focus attention on an all but forgotten 30 year-old loophole in Texas law that was allowing massive amounts of preventable industrial pollution.

Although the Texas Clean Air Act was passed in 1971, the law did not cover industrial facilities that were already in operation at the time.[83] Unlike facilities that were to be built later, these older and dirtier "grandfathered" facilities were allowed to continue to operate without the best available pollution control technology and without public hearings on the impacts of their pollution on the health of people in surrounding neighborhoods. In theory, these "grandfathered" plants had to apply for permits, if they chose to expand or significantly change their operations.

Grandfathered facilities were exempted from the law in 1971 because it was believed they would either become obsolete and close down or upgrade their operations and get permits at a later date. By late 1996, it was clear that this was not happening. Because of poor oversight by the state agency, changes in operations were rarely identified. Consequently, few polluters had their grandfathered status revoked. Under questioning from the legislature, the state environmental agency was unable to say how many grandfathered facilities there were.[84] As a result Texas lawmakers instructed the state environmental agency to conduct a survey in 1997 to determine exactly how many grandfathered facilities there were in Texas. The large number of grandfathered facilities found to be still in operation was shocking.

When the State environmental agency finally took the trouble to look, they found what many environmental activists suspected. Over 800 grandfathered facilities still enjoyed the legal loophole that allowed 36% of all Texas' industrial pollution to escape critical government regulations. Put in perspective, these facilities contributed a whopping 903,800 tons of pollutants to the air – in a single year.[85] This is as much ozone pollution-causing chemicals as 18 million automobiles (there are about 9 million in Texas).[86] By 1999, almost 30 years after the Texas Clean Air Act was passed, almost half of the state's 1,648 industrial plants enjoyed some sort of exemption.

## Is This Any Way to Treat Our Children?

What does air pollution from grandfathered polluters mean for children in Texas? A report by the Sustainable Energy & Economic Development Coalition revealed the following facts[87]:

- Over 225,000 children attend schools located in close proximity to facilities that emit over 300,000 tons of smog-forming pollution each year.

- In seven of the 29 Texas counties there is unsafe air hovering over 292 schools. These schools are located within a two-mile radius of a major grandfathered polluter.

- More than one-third (107) of these at-risk schools are within two miles of multiple plants, a situation that increases the exposure of children to harmful pollutants.

## Back-Room Politics and Campaign Cash

Why has the obvious public health threat caused by grandfathered facilities escaped the attention of Texas lawmakers for so long? Following the money helps to explain why. Public Research Works evaluated the influence of campaign contributions over the legislative process and identified $10,216,454 in political expenditures from the grandfathered interests to candidates for elected office from 1993 to 1998. Public Research Works tracked a total of 138 contributors representing 57 parent companies. These contributors gave $4,649,885 in the period from 1993 to 1998 to Governor George W. Bush and Lt. Governor Rick Perry and current members of the Texas Legislature.

In fact, every single member of the Legislature and both the Governor and Lt. Governor have received campaign contributions directly from the company PACs of the top 100 grandfathered air polluters.[88]

When George W. Bush took office in 1995, public concern and media attention to air pollution problems was growing. An enlightened public no longer tolerated dirty air as 'the smell of money.' As citizens across Texas began organizing to close the loophole for grandfathered polluters, Governor Bush and the heads of chemical plants, refineries and power plants began their efforts to keep the loophole open.

With impending EPA deadlines for cleaner air and the possibility of legislative action to close the loophole, Governor Bush and his 'partnership' of industry representatives began holding secret meetings to come up with a plan to keep the loophole open.[89] Internal documents, which would later come to light, revealed the goal of Bush's partnership was to appease the public and minimize cost to industry.

In the best of worlds, public policy is determined after the opportunity for public input and debate. This was not the case when the Governor decided to respond to the growing air pollution crisis in Texas. The actions of George W. Bush and his appointees reveal a controversial method of governing and his loyalty to powerful business interests.

The true story behind Governor Bush's actions only came to light in early 1999 after an environmental group obtained hidden documents through a formal request under the Public Information Act.[90] A lawsuit was filed alleging that Governor Bush and State Agencies failed to turn over all documents.[91] In 1996 some state regulators were actually considering closing the loophole for grandfathered polluters and requiring mandatory compliance with the Texas Clean Air Act. Instead, Governor Bush asked oil and gas industry leaders to draft a proposal which would allow voluntary, rather than mandatory compliance.

In secret meetings between industry representatives, state regulators and sometimes the Governor's staff agreed to the basics of the "voluntary program" that would later become Texas law. The program would allow grandfathered facilities to voluntarily obtain permits *if* they wanted. It would allow them to do so without making significant investments in pollution controls or reductions in air pollution. Companies who participated in these private meetings to shape public policy, made, and would make, major contributions to Bush's election campaigns.

The first of these meetings took place in December of 1996, when Ralph Marquez, Governor Bush's first appointee to the TNRCC, called eleven major industry representatives together for a private meeting where the future of grandfathered industries was discussed. Governor Bush's appointment of Marquez helped to insure industry's easy access to the state houses of government. Marquez had worked for 30 years with the Monsanto Chemical Company, and he worked with the

Texas Chemical Council, a powerful industry lobby association.

Minutes of the secret meetings show that some TNRCC officials were considering legislation to force the outdated grandfathered plants to upgrade pollution equipment and reduce emissions. After industry objected, the governor's environmental policy director called Governor Bush informing him that, "Industry has expressed concern that the TNRCC is moving too quickly and may rashly seek legislation this session."[92]

A TNRCC attorney attending the January 1997 meetings with industry representatives described their position on grandfathered pollution, " they certainly don't think it's a problem." The memo also makes clear industry's reluctance to do anything about their grandfathered pollution. The memo describes the attitude of industry representatives, "the general reaction from some of the more powerful groups (Texas Association of Business, Texas Mid-Continent Oil & Gas Association, the Utilities) is, 'why now, why so fast, why at all?'"[93]

## The Tail Wags the Dog
## Polluters Decide Environmental Policy

The answer to the question, "why at all," was simple. The public was demanding that something be done about air pollution. Instead of insuring an open process that allowed for public input into a critically important public policy decision, Governor Bush *simply asked the industry responsible for pollution, to design the policy.*[94] In coordination with the Governor's office, representatives from Exxon and Marathon Oil developed a "voluntary pollution abatement program" that would close the loophole on paper without requiring industry to make a significant reduction in air pollution.

In April of 1997, Governor Bush's office sent Exxon's and Marathon's first proposal for the voluntary program to TNRCC Commissioner Ralph Marquez[95] The proposal did not require companies to meet state pollution standards. Instead, it made the program for grandfathered polluters voluntary, allowing a grace period for companies that chose to take part.

In June of 1997, after further work in private and still with no involvement or input from public representatives, Exxon and Marathon presented the policy proposal Governor Bush had asked them to prepare. It was presented to a group of 40 industry representatives, including plant managers, presidents, vice-presidents, and CEO's of the State's largest grandfathered polluters.[96] Governor Bush's environmental policy advisor was in attendance.[97]

The notes of Jim Kennedy, an industry representative from DuPont who attended the June meeting, make it clear that the relationship between industry and the Bush Administration was one of 'the tail wagging the dog.' The presentation of the Exxon/Marathon policy proposal for grandfathered polluters was characterized as, "This is the way it's going to be - do you want to get on board or not?" The proposal was also described as, "something that has been agreed to at high levels and was not subject to change."[98]

The DuPont representative also wrote, "Clearly, the "insiders" from oil & gas believe that the Governor's office will persuade the TNRCC to accept whatever program is developed between the industry group and the Governor's office."[99] Such statements, which were never intended for public disclosure, only confirmed what environmental organizations had been saying for years. The environmental agency of Texas, run by the Governor's appointees, was firmly in industry's pocket.

Notes of the secret meetings also make it clear that the voluntary program was never intended to significantly reduce pollution. The notes state that industry's proposal for the program, "had no meat with respect to actual emissions." The DuPont representative observed, "One of the leaders actually stated that emission reduction was not a primary driver for the program."[100]

The deliberate exclusion of public representatives in this closed-door process was clearly no accident. The Dupont representative wrote that there had been a discussion about the possibility of public involvement. However, according to his notes, "This thought was pretty much dismissed-I believe mainly because the leadership doesn't have any real value for public involvement." Clearly, the "leadership" didn't want public involvement because it was understood that the public, if allowed to participate in the process, would have insisted on a program with the primary goal of reducing emissions.

As is too often the case, public input was only to be allowed in this environmental policy issue *after* important decisions had already been made. It was also decided at the meetings to set up another committee at a later date, this time *with* public representatives, so they could "tweak it (the voluntary plan) a little bit and approve it."[101] This was done in September of 1997 when Texas Natural Resources Commission, run by Governor Bush's appointees, formed the "Clean Air Responsibility Committee (CARE)." The public was told the CARE committee, now with public participation, would develop a "voluntary program" to reduce pollution from grandfathered industrial facilities. The public was never told that for eight months, industry representatives, state regulators, and on some occasions, the Governor's staff, had already been meeting to develop the program.

To make sure the CARE committee was going to do what Governor Bush's "partnership" wanted, the committee was stacked with seven industry representatives and only four from citizen/environmental groups. The committee proceeded to have only one public hearing for the entire state. It was scheduled in the morning on a workday—at a location in Austin far from the cities and communities suffering the most from industrial air pollution. This insured that industry lobbyists, more so than pollution victims, would attend the meeting to testify.

On October 21, 1997, Texans United Education Fund, wrote Governor Bush and his TNRCC appointees a letter requesting that the CARE Committee be enlarged to include more public representatives—and that hearings be held in areas where industrial pollution was a serious problem. TNRCC refused the requests and Governor Bush never bothered to acknowledge, much less answer the letter.

Since the Governor and his environmental agency appointees would not open their official process to allow for adequate public involvement, Texans United and other environmental groups decided to sponsor public hearings where citizens could be heard. A group of air pollution experts, including former environmental agency investigators, was empanelled to hold public hearings at courthouses in two different sites near Houston's polluted Ship Channel communities. Although the EPA, elected officials, and the media attended the public hearings, the Governor's office and the TNRCC ignored invitations to attend. What they missed was what they didn't want to hear. Overwhelming testimony described the suffering caused by air pollution and a public outcry over the need to close the loophole for grandfathered polluters.

As predicted, the TNRCC's CARE Committee rubber-stamped the voluntary program that had already been shaped in closed-door meetings with industry heavyweights. The vote was exactly as predicted, with seven industry representatives voting for the program and all four public representatives voting to reject it. A minority report issued by public representatives of CARE, accused industry members of failing to consider public testimony and refusing even to recognize that air pollution from grandfathered facilities was a problem.  Governor Bush ignored the minority report, made his support for the voluntary program public, and it became official state regulatory policy.

## The Voluntary Violators

A few months later, in November of 1997, Governor Bush met together with the first ten companies to symbolically join his voluntary program at a news conference on the Houston Ship Channel, home to the largest concentration of chemical plants and refineries in the nation.   One of these ten companies was Crown Central Petroleum, one of the most notorious polluters in the state.  Although over a third of this oil refinery's 3,700 tons of air pollution each year was from its grandfathered facilities.[102]  Like the other companies, Crown stood beside the governor and pledged to reduce its pollution.  It made the promise without saying how, how much, or when these reductions would happen.  Crown's chief executive officer contributed to both of Bush's gubernatorial campaigns and he and his wife made the maximum allowable contribution to Bush's Presidential Campaign.[103] Crown's Political Action Committee and lobbyists donated $41,000 to Governor Bush's gubernatorial campaigns between 1993 and 1998.[104]

After the news conference with the Governor, a list of the Governor's "volunteers", including Crown, was sent to the Houston-Galveston Area Council and Houston Mayor Lee Brown by the Texas Natural Resource Conservation Commission.  These "volunteers" were then presented a "Clean Air Action Award" at a "Regional Clean Air Summit" extravaganza which was attended by elected officials, TNRCC commissioners, the EPA and, of course, representatives from industry.

The fact that Crown was a blatant, repeat pollution law violator didn't seem to matter.  Completely ignored by the taxpayer funded Clean Air Summit, was the fact that Crown had amassed thousands of hours of Clean Air Act violations and had a major air pollution event nearly every month in the years 1996 and 1997.  These events totaled nearly 1,000 tons of excess sulfur dioxide in only two years time.[105]

After Crown joined Governor Bush's "voluntary" program in late 1997, Clean Air Act violations reached their highest rate in two years during the first three months of 1998.  In fact, at the same time Crown received their "Clean Air Action Award," in June of 1998, which thanked them for helping people to "breathe easier," the company was under enforcement action by the TNRCC because of violations and was the target of two highly publicized citizen lawsuits.  Crown was being sued in federal court for thousands of Clean Air Act violations,[106] and in state court by nearby residents who claimed property and health damages as a result of its grossly negligent air pollution.[107]  Additionally, Crown was involved in a bitter labor dispute after it locked-out the experienced union workers at the plant and replaced them with contract workers.[108]  What didn't seem to matter to the government bureaucrats, was that Crown was making the air *dirtier* and harder to breathe.  Some felt the government's insensitivity was related to the fact that neighboring communities were predominately Hispanic and working class.

The Governor's message to Crown and other industrial polluters was clear.  Even if companies violated the law and polluted the community—they could still be rewarded, just by participating in his "voluntary" program.  The more subtle message, whether intended or not, was that companies could expect the state agency to go easy on them when it came to enforcing the law.

Crown's continuing violations after it received the "Clean Air Action Award" led to EPA enforcement action and the case being forwarded to the Department of Justice. Because of public outrage over Crown's violations, the TNRCC finally took action against the company in August of 1998. Crown was made to pay the largest air pollution fine in Texas history.[109] The fine however, did not take into account Crown's economic benefit from the years of violations. Because of this, the TNRCC was sued in state court and a formal civil rights complaint was filed with the EPA against the agency.

In March of 1998, Gov. Bush announced that a total of 36 companies had joined the voluntary program and, as a result, 25,000 tons of the 900,000 tons of grandfathered industrial air emissions in Texas would be cut. However, *"Too Little-Too Late,"* a study released in November of 1998 by the Environmental Defense Fund, revealed that the companies were not keeping their promises to reduce pollution and, even if they did, only a 3% reduction of all the grandfathered air pollution would be achieved.

Crown Petroleum is an example of why Governor Bush's "voluntary program" is a failure. As of November 1998, a year after Crown joined the voluntary program, Crown still hadn't committed to taking specific actions to reduce pollution. Crown said it was waiting on the state agency to make rules for a voluntary program. However, the state agency, run by Bush's appointees, said it was waiting on the legislature to pass a law before it would issue regulations.[110] In fact, there was nothing to prevent Crown or other companies from going ahead with actions to reduce pollution. It was, after all, a voluntary program. Apparently, it was cheaper to run business as usual, and wait for regulations that might identify an economic incentive.

Because of public outrage over Crown's long standing and continuing violations, the state environmental agency finally acted in August of 1998 and made Crown, one of Governor Bush's first volunteers, pay the largest air pollution fine in Texas history."[111] Governor Bush's appointees refused to assess a fine that considered Crown's economic benefits from years of violations.

## The Texas Legislature Caves In

In 1999 the Texas Legislature passed two laws covering grandfathered facilities, both of which Governor Bush signed. For Governor Bush and his industry supporters, the legislative battle was a close call.

Citizen organizations had mounted an effective grassroots campaign to close the grandfathered loophole. Every major newspaper in Texas had editorialized against Bush's concept of voluntary compliance before the votes were taken. The titles often told the story; "Texas needs to quit coddling polluter," (*Austin American Statesman*); "Clean Air, Legislature should close loophole for older plants, " (*Dallas Morning News*); "Clamp Down on Polluters," (*El Paso Times*).[112] Newspaper editors, like many of their readers, felt that it was unfair to require some companies to clean up their emissions and incur the cost of compliance, when other companies could choose not to comply and operate more cheaply. It was also unfair to force citizens to make sacrifices to clean up the air while certain industrial polluters were allowed the option of conducting business-as-usual.

One of the two laws concerning grandfathered facilities signed by Governor Bush covered chemical plants, refineries, and some other large industrial polluters. The other law he signed concerned grandfathered facilities at power companies. The law for chemical plants and refineries continued the loophole and the "voluntary" program. However, at the end of the legislative session, Governor Bush was forced to strike a compromise on grandfathered facilities at power plants. These facilities were required to reduce emissions.

The Bush Presidential campaign, now focuses on the legislation he signed which "mandated" pollution reductions from power plants as a major "success story." In fact, Bush had steadfastly backed the "voluntary" concept for utility companies for more than two years. The campaign has little to say about the "voluntary" program for chemical plants and refineries.

George W. Bush claims that the air pollution laws he signed were passed with "bipartisan support." In fact, a small number of Democrats on a key conference committee did cave in to pressure and passed the bill that embodied Bush's voluntary program for chemical plants and refineries. Texas environmental organizations described the law as weak and with a loophole full of loopholes. Political insiders say Texas lawmakers, who were reluctant to leave the grandfathered pollution loophole open, simply didn't want to cross a popular Governor on his way to becoming President.

What ultimately came out of the Texas legislature was a bipartisan *failure* to address a serious environmental and public health problem. Holding true to his belief in economic incentives for industry, the law signed by Governor Bush gave amnesty to companies whose grandfathered facilities have been operating illegally without a permit. They only had to join the voluntary program.[113]

George W. Bush touted the law as a significant accomplishment of his administration. In fact, in a *New York Times* story he says, "'I'm the person who initiated the discussions, I'm the person who asked industry to get into compliance, and they did." However, EPA officials confirmed that emissions reductions brought about by the law were not sufficient to bring Texas' major metropolitan areas into compliance with federal ozone standards.

In August of 2000, Crown Central Petroleum, one of Governor's Bush's first ten volunteers, was again facing a record pollution fine for even more air pollution violations.

# Following the Money
## *Grandfathered Polluters Bet Big on Bush*

Public Research Works, a nonprofit, environmental research and education organization in Texas, said the companies that attended the secret meetings to develop the basics of the voluntary program were among Bush's most reliable and generous contributors. At least $973,000 in presidential campaign contributions was traced to employees or family members of the companies attending the meetings, or to lawyers and lobbyists who represent the companies.

Marathon's former President Beghini and A.L. Condray of Exxon, who both attended the secret meetings, and asked by Bush to draft proposals for the voluntary program. Mr. Beghini gave the maximum $1,000 contribution allowed to the Bush campaign, as did his wife. Exxon's Political Action Committee was also a major contributor to Bush. At least nine of Mr. Bush's "Pioneers," who pledged to raise at least $100,000 for his campaign effort, are connected to the companies participating in the secret meetings.

In a *New York Times* story about Bush and his support of pollution legislation, a Bush campaign spokesman stated that the governor did not make decisions based on campaign contributions but on "what is best for Texas." He also said that the industry representative's characterization of the June 19 meeting on grandfathered pollution "was not accurate." Although the person who wrote the notes about the meeting could not be reached for comment and Exxon officials declined to comment, a Marathon Oil spokesman said his company frequently met with state and local officials to discuss environmental policy.

## Polluters Bet Big on Bush for Governor

Grandfathered industrial polluters donated large sums during both of Governor Bush's campaigns for Governor. Political Action Committees (PACs) and lobbyists of the top 100 grandfathered polluters and others that participated in secret meetings to develop the voluntary compliance program donated more than $670,000 to Governor Bush's gubernatorial campaigns.

These participants include some of the largest industrial polluters in the state, such as Texas Utilities, Dow Chemical, Lyondell Petrochemical, Alcoa, Exxon, and many others.

| Company Political Action Committee | $ Contributed to G.W..Bush Gubernatorial Campaigns 1993-1998 | Secret Meetings Participant |
|---|---|---|
| Alcoa | $2,000 | x |
| Apache Corporation | $1,000 | |
| ARCO | $13,250 | |
| Assn. of Electric Companies of TX | $1,500 | x |
| BP Amoco | $5,000 | x |
| Central and Southwest Corp/ American Electric Power Co | $18,500 | x |
| Champion International Corp | $5,250 | |
| Coastal Corp | $37,250 | x |
| Crown Central Petroleum Corp | $6,000 | |
| Dow Chemical Company | $26,000 | |
| Duke Capital Corp | $23,000 | |
| Eastman Chemical Company | $7,200 | x |
| El Paso Energy Corp. | $6,000 | |
| Enron Corp | $30,000 | |
| Entergy Gulf States | $9,500 | x |
| Exxon | $24,200 | x |
| Fulbright & Jaworski | $67,000 | x |

| Company Political Action Committee | $ Contributed to G.W..Bush Gubernatorial Campaigns 1993-1998 | Secret Meetings Participant |
|---|---|---|
| International Paper | $5,000 | |
| Hired Gun Lobbyists | $150,500 | |
| Koch Industries | $4,500 | |
| Lockheed | $17,400 | x |
| Lyondell Petrochemical GP Inc. | $3,500 | x |
| MND Energy Corporation | $2,250 | |
| Mobil Oil | $250 | x |
| New Century Energies | $2,000 | |
| Oryx Energy Company | $3,000 | |
| PG & E | $5,000 | |
| Phillips/GPM | $11,998 | x |
| Rohm & Haas | $2,000 | |
| Southwestern Electric ServiceCo. | $6,250 | |
| Tenneco, Inc. | $1,000 | |
| Texaco Inc | $20,000 | x |
| Texas Utilities | $64,800 | x |
| Torch Energy Marketing | $2,400 | |
| TX Assn. of Business & Commerce PAC | $20,000 | x |
| TX Cattle Feeders Assn./BEEF | $20,000 | x |
| TX Cotton Ginners Assn. PAC | $500 | x |
| TX Mid-Continent Oil & Gas | $18,000 | x |
| Ultramar Diamond Shamrock | $5,000 | |
| Union Carbide | $3,500 | |
| Union Pacific Resources | $11,000 | |
| Valero Refining | $30,000 | |
| **TOTAL** | **$692,498** | |

(Source: Public Research Works).


According to a study conducted by the *Los Angeles Times*, Governor Bush received $1.5 million from 55 grandfathered companies when contributions by executives were also factored into the equation.114    The largest contributor is Enron Corporation, a leading energy company, whose representatives and their agents donated $384,559.    Enron board member Kenneth Lay personally gave the Governor $76,000 from 1993 to 1998.

Sterling Chemical's political action committee was the second largest contributor with $239,000 during the same period.    Virgil Waggoner, Sterling Chemicals Vice-Chairman personally gave $85,000 to George W. Bush's campaigns for governor.

In discussing the enthusiasm that the chemical industry has for Governor Bush, the head of a major trade association was quoted in the *Washington Post* to say, "This industry has openly said we're going to support Bush and [is] committing to raise a huge sum of money for him."[115] The chemical industry proceeded to do just that.

## Polluters Bet Big on Bush for President

While the Texas Legislature debated closing the grandfather loophole, Governor Bush announced his intention to run for President, and his campaign was financially jump-started by the same grandfathered industries.    In just his first months of fund-raising, Presidential candidate Bush raised more than $313,000 dollars from representatives of 32 of the top 100 grandfathered industrial polluters.

The analysis by Public Research Works showed that 25 of the top 30 grandfathered polluters contributed $463,312 to the presidential campaign.  These firms emit more than 694,000 tons of grandfathered air pollution annually[116]

In July, after Bush signed the "voluntary pollution permitting program" into law, the Bush Presidential campaign announced that it had shattered all fund-raising records with a total from national contributors of over $37 million dollars. By the end of June, the top 100 grandfathered interests and the secret meeting participants (in Texas alone) had contributed more than $976,000 to Bush's presidential coffers.

The Governor's top contributor to his presidential campaign is the law firm Vinson & Elkins. As of September 1, 1999 it had contributed $184,850. Vinson & Elkins represents Alcoa Inc., which has the single largest source of grandfathered emissions in the Texas, discharging over 100,000 tons of pollution annually.[117] Alcoa was not covered by the two pieces of legislation passed in 1999 to address grandfathered air polluters. Vinson & Elkins also represented other big time Texas polluters.

The Enron Corporation, which has also been a generous contributor to Gov. Bush's gubernatorial races, has given $103,100 to his presidential campaign. They are followed by the law firm Baker & Botts, which lobbies on behalf of eight grandfathered polluters and has contributed $82,550 to the presidential campaign. Baker & Botts' client list includes the grandfathered polluters: Huntsman Petrochemical, Rohm & Haas, Goodyear Tire & Rubber, Amoco Oil, Mobil Oil, Shell Oil, Union Carbide, and Valero Refining.

Texas Utilities (TU) produces the most grandfathered pollution: 247,000 tons of chemicals in the air, from more than 20 facilities.[118] TU also contributed heavily with over $42,000 from staff, directors, and their spouses. In addition, the law firm which represents TU on air pollution issues alone gave an additional $9000 to the Presidential campaign.

| Company PACS | Contributions to Presidential Campaign March thru June 1999 | Secret Meeting Participant | Tons of Grandfathered emissions annually |
|---|---|---|---|
| 3M Company | $1,000 | | 892 |
| Alcoa | $1,000 | x | 104,304 |
| Anadark0 | $6,000 | | 814 |
| Apache Corp. | $2,000 | | 1395 |
| ARCO | $6,250 | | 1942 |
| Baker & Botts* (lobbyists who do work for many Grand- fathered polluters) | $82,550 | | |
| BASF | $2,000 | x | |
| Bayer Corporation | $5,500 | | 1054 |
| BP Amoco | $8,500 | x | 12,772 |
| Cabot Oil & Gas Corp. | $4,000 | | 54,052 |
| Central & Southwest /Amer.ElectricPower | $8,000 | x | 20,022 |
| Chevron | $18,000 | | 1834 |
| City Public Service of San Antonio | $250 | x | 4455 |
| Coastal Corp | $10,250 | x | 8999 |
| Conoco | $9,250 | | 1000 |
| Degussa Corp. | $1,950 | | 24,614 |
| Dow | $22,650 | | 6222 |
| Duke | $8,000 | | 18,017 |
| DuPont | $2,000 | x | |
| Dynegy Inc | $13,250 | | 25,311 |
| Eastman Chemical | $19,425 | x | 4919 |
| El Paso Electric | $1,000 | | 3091 |
| El Paso Energy | $39,884 | | 12,189 |
| El Paso Field Services | $1,000 | | 2597 |
| Elf Atochem NA Inc | $6,000 | x | 946 |
| Enron | $103,100 | | 6609 |
| Entergy/Gulf States Utilities | $4,000 | x | 9753 |

| Company PACS | Contributions to Presidential Campaign March thru June 1999 | Secret Meeting Participant | Tons of Grandfathered emissions annually |
|---|---|---|---|
| Equilon Enterprises | $2,000 | | 4061 |
| Equistar Chemicals | $3,200 | | 2082 |
| Exxon | $19,250 | x | 30,660 |
| Fina Inc. | $14,250 | x | 1532 |
| Fulbright & Jaworski | $8,450 | x | |
| Goodyear Tire & Rubber | $2,000 | x | 2344 |
| Hired Guns (more than one Grand-fathered polluter client) | $11,750 | | |
| Hoechst Celanese | $8,150 | | 2375 |
| Houston Industries/ Reliant Energy | $43,753 | x | 974 |
| Huntsman Corp | $1,000 | x | 3677 |
| International Paper | $3,250 | | 712 |
| Koch Industries | $30,400 | | 9172 |
| Lockheed | $10,250 | x | |
| Lone Star Steel | $4,000 | | 910 |
| Louisiana PacificCorp | $250 | | 8779 |
| Lyondell | $4,000 | x | 3267 |
| Mitchell Energy/ MND Energy Corp. | $1,000 | | 2055 |
| Mobil | $14,000 | x | 34,261 |
| Monsanto/Solutia | $1,500 | x | |
| Occidental Chemical | $23,850 | | 694 |
| PG&E | $3,250 | | 5950 |
| Phillips/GPM | $11,500 | x | 4368 |
| Pioneer Natural Resource Co. | $3,000 | | 1222 |
| Reynolds Metals | $2,000 | | 3010 |
| Rohm & Haas | $7,000 | | 2464 |
| Shell Oil | $25,650 | x | 11,633 |

| Company PACS | Contributions to Presidential Campaign March thru June 1999 | Secret Meeting Participant | Tons of Grandfathered emissions annually |
|---|---|---|---|
| Sid Richardson Carbon Blk/Bass Companies | $15,000 | | 2017 |
| Temple Inland Forest Products | $12,500 | x | 988 |
| Tenneco | $12,000 | | 1129 |
| Texaco Inc | $6,500 | x | 5197 |
| Texas Utilities/Enserch | $42,000 | x | 247,089 |
| Tx & South-western Cattle Raisers PAC | $3,898 | x | |
| Ultramar Diamond Shamrock | $10,250 | | 4586 |
| Union Carbide | $2,000 | | 8558 |
| Union Pacific Resources | $22,000 | | 5378 |
| Unocal | $3,750 | | 2641 |
| Valero Refining | $6,500 | | 2688 |
| Vinson & Elkins* (law firm for Alcoa on air pollution matters) | $184,850 | | |
| Vintage Petroleum | $250 | | 2809 |
| Worsham, Forsythe & Wooldridge (law firm forTexas Utilities on air pollution matters) | $9,000 | | |
| **TOTAL** | **$976,010** | **Tons Pollution** | **761,085** |

Source: Public Research Works and Center for Responsive Politics.
* Totals for Vinson & Elkins and Baker and Botts include contributions as of September 1, 1999.

     The analysis by Public Research Works showed that 25 of the top 30 grandfathered polluters contributed

$463,312 to the presidential campaign. These firms emit more than 694,000 tons of grandfathered air pollution annually[119]

## The Real Cost of Campaign Contributions

Campaign contributions from polluters are investments that pay off when they bring about governmental decisions that keep them from having to spend money on such things as pollution controls. If campaign contributions result in weak enforcement by government agencies, then money is also saved on pollution fines that don't have to be paid.

Companies can save more money than they give and public officials get money to feather their nests and further their careers. Unfortunately, citizens who are left to live with the pollution can end up paying a terrible price. That price is often measured in increased health care costs and loss of property values. It is also reflected in the loss of quality of life and sometimes the loss of life, neither of which can be measured in dollar amounts.

A May 1996 report by the Natural Resources Defense Council estimated that Texas power plants emit particulates that are responsible for 2,617 premature deaths of Texans each year.[120] An April 1999 study conducted for the city of Houston on the health effects of air pollution found that 435 people die prematurely every year because of air pollution. In addition, if the region cleaned up its air it would save about $2.9 to $3.1 billion annually in health care costs[121]

An October 1999 study calculated that statewide health impacts of high ozone levels in Texas found 6200 hospital admissions and 14,500 emergency room visits for respiratory and cardio-vascular hospital admissions associated with high ozone levels. In addition, the ozone levels resulted in an estimated 42,000 cases of shortness of breath and 660,000 asthma attacks.[122]

Governor Bush's philosophy of relying on weak "voluntary" programs, gave the big polluters and campaign contributors exactly what they wanted. It provided them with valuable public relations rhetoric without requiring any substantial effort or reduction in pollution. Unfortunately, average Texans are paying the price and don't even know it.

# Avoiding Accountability
## *Secrecy for Environmental Audits*

Two of the main criticisms of George W. Bush's environmental policy have been the lack of disclosure related to agency enforcement actions and the lack of accountability for companies found guilty of unlawful pollution. A glaring example of the Bush administration's leniency toward pollution violators and his quick forgiveness of their wrongdoing, was the 1995 Texas Environmental Health and Safety Audit Privilege Act which he signed into law.

The unstated purpose of the law was to reduce industry's exposure to fines and penalties. An advertisement for an industry sponsored workshop on The Texas Audit Privilege Act stated, "Make sure you know how to reduce your exposure to fines and penalties when you conduct an audit." When advertising a workshop on the Texas Risk Reduction Rules, it said, "Discover how to use the TRRP rules to save your company money."[123]

The original version of the law was largely written by the Texas Chemical Council lobbyist Kinnan Goleman.[124] The law was dubbed by its critics as, "the polluter immunity law" because it created sweeping protections for polluters that performed internal environmental or safety audits within their own facilities. In short, the law made such audits "privileged," and prevented their use, even in criminal prosecutions conducted by State or local authorities. Polluters were immune from responsibility for violations which they discovered (or disclosed) in their self-conducted audits.[125]

Between May of 1995, when Governor Bush signed the legislation, and October 1999, companies in Texas conducted 1040 of these "privileged" audits. Violations have been almost 25 percent of the time and, likewise, the companies have received immunity, for what were usually multiple violations, on 246 occasions.

If dollars indicate level of interest, polluter immunity legislation held a high priority for many of Governor Bush's close supporters in the oil, natural gas, chemical, electronics, electric utility, manufacturing and factory farming industries. Corporate interests that were represented by groups lobbying for audit privilege legislation, contributed more than $4 million to Bush's two gubernatorial campaign[126]

Supporters of the legislation argued that granting immunity and privilege for internal audits gave companies the needed incentive to clean up their operations. It also allowed them to do so without fear of being held responsible for any violations the audits revealed. Supporters rationalized that fear of potential liability would otherwise discourage companies from voluntarily evaluating their problems and taking steps to correct them. Without immunity for violations, supporters of the legislation admitted that companies might be tempted to whitewash their problems or look the other way.

Although the sponsor of the legislation, State Representative Warren Chisum, repeatedly assured the House that the purpose of the bill wasn't "to protect bad actors," others however, weren't so sure.[127]

Prosecutors and environmentalists argued that the legislation set a bad example and would allow polluters to escape accountability when they clearly had violated environmental or health and safety laws. The audit privilege law only served to reward polluters for complying with state law, which was something they were already required, morally and legally, to do anyway.

Kate Kelly, of the Travis County Attorney's office, testified before the House Environmental Affairs

Committee that the bill gave polluters more rights than other criminal defendants. Likewise, a representative of the Harris County District Attorney's Office expressed concern that companies would use the law as a shield, conveniently performing an audit immediately after every serious pollution event so that they would be provided full and complete immunity.

Of almost greater concern was that the law denied audit information, not only to prosecutors and the general public, but also to victims who suffered damages as a result of environmental negligence and illegal pollution. People harmed by a polluter's violation of an environmental law who sued for damages would often find that a privileged audit report contained the only direct evidence of a violation.[128]  As such, the audit evidence could not be used to prove the injured victim's right to relief.

Environmental audits often uncover information that the public has a right and need to know. Many chemical plants and refineries handle extremely hazardous, often volatile, substances. Moreover, many of these facilities are located in the heart of residential neighborhoods. The public must be notified of reoccurring problems and dangerous conditions at the facility, especially if those conditions might present possible dangers to nearby communities. Without knowing the deficiencies, communities find it impossible to determine if a hazardous condition has been corrected.

The polluter immunity law signed by Governor Bush undermines the principles upon which our community-right-to-know laws are based. In the early 1990's Texans United negotiated "Good Neighbor Agreements" with several chemical plants and refineries that actually provided for citizen participation in environmental and safety audits. Governor Bush's signing of the audit privilege law helped give companies an excuse to avoid accountability to the public, and to refuse the communities request for full, fair and often critical disclosure.

Companies that have taken advantage of these immunity statutes are among the largest pollution generators in the state including, Exxon, ALCOA, Union Carbide, ARCO Permian, Sterling Chemicals, Bell Helicopters, Chemical Waste Management, Enron, Texas Instruments, Elf Atochem, and many others.

The EPA and various Texas environmental groups demanded that provisions of the polluter immunity law be changed. In fact, the EPA even threatened to strip Texas of its authority to administer several licensing and enforcement functions on behalf of the federal government if Texas did not rescind parts of its new law. The initial demands by the EPA included the following conditions:

- Texas must eliminate application of immunity and privilege provisions to criminal actions.

- Texas must eliminate application of immunity where a violation results in a serious threat to health or the environment, or where the violator has obtained a substantial economic benefit that gives it a competitive advantage.

- Texas must clarify that the privilege does not impair access to information that is required to be made available to the public under existing federal or state law.

Under pressure from the EPA, the Legislature and the Governor entered into closed-door negotiations with the EPA concerning amendments to the legislation. In March of 1997, two months into the legislative session, a compromise agreement was finally reached.[129] Although the EPA had backed down on some of its demands, "2/3 of the problem" was rectified.[130]

Governor Bush appointees at the TNRCC were furious that the EPA had tinkered with their polluter immunity law. TNRCC Chairman Barry McBee flew to Washington, D.C. and complained to the U.S. Senate about the EPA's demands for changes to Texas' polluter immunity legislation. He complained bitterly about a "paternalistic-parent child relationship" between the EPA and the states, which (he felt) was "not healthy."

McBee accused the EPA of overstepping its regulatory authority and called on Congress to enact federal polluter immunity legislation. That did not occur. In fact, despite the Bush administrations' loud protests, both the EPA and the Department of Justice remained "deeply opposed to audit privileges in any form."[131]

## Promoting Compliance or Cover-up?

Polluter immunity legislation was a boondoggle for many of Texas's biggest polluters who were and remain some of the biggest check writers to the "Bush for President" campaign. Records reveal that companies that are contributors to Governor Bush directly or indirectly have used the immunity law far more frequently than others. Of the 242 companies that submitted privileged audits, forty-five (45), or slightly less than 20 percent, were companies whose political action committees or employees contributed to Bush's gubernatorial campaigns. That same 20 percent group of contributors accounted for 48 percent of all requests for immunity made necessary by violations found in these same audits. In other words, companies pushing the legislation (and contributing to the governor) were collectively among the worst polluters which had the most to gain by cloaking their violations in privilege.[132]

Just as opponents of the polluter immunity law had feared, the law has been used to shield violators from responsibility for their bad acts and to hide the substance of these violations from the public. These citizens need to know about the risks that face their communities on a day in, day out basis.

One example occurred in the summer of 1995, when the University of Texas at Arlington conducted an audit and investigation to determine whether students, faculty, and staff had been exposed to air-borne asbestos fibers in campus buildings.[133] Asbestos has been strongly linked to specific types of cancer and other health risks. Although the investigation had been prompted by a whistle-blower who claimed that the university endangered people by violating state and federal laws, the Texas Attorney General still ruled that the information, uncovered through the audit, should be kept secret under the Texas Public Information Act. The university claimed that there was a privilege for information obtained via the audit—even though a whistle-blower had alerted the university and the public that the problem existed. Incredibly, the law allowed information of the asbestos violations to be kept secret, even from discovery in civil lawsuits brought over health effects to students, etc., which had resulted from the university's dangerous conditions.

In legislative hearings, Representative Warren Chisum, chair of the Texas House of Representatives' Environmental Regulation Committee, insisted that the audit privilege law would not allow polluters to perform an audit, after the fact in, order to cover up bad acts. However, that's exactly what appears to have happened at the university. A whistle-blower squawked, a suit was filed, an audit was performed, and information was concealed. In the final analysis, the Texas audit privilege law did little more than allow another Texas polluter to evade public disclosure and reduce its potential for successful civil prosecution.

Without the public being allowed to see the 1,000-plus audits which have been done under this law, or to know the details of the hundreds of environmental violations that have been, or will be pardoned, the full consequences on the public health and the environment may never be known.

### Following the Money: Bush Contributors
### Back Audit Privilege Law

Those companies who actively supported Texas' audit privilege legislation historically have also been among Governor Bush's most generous campaign contributors.

At the House Environmental Regulation Committee hearing on April 25, 1996, the following businesses and industry groups actively lobbied for the pollution immunity bill:

- American Electronics Association
- Association of Electric Companies of Texas (investor-owned utility group)
- Eastman Chemical/Texas Eastman
- General Motors Corporation
- Monarch Paint Company
- Texas Assoc. of Business and Chambers of Commerce
- Texas Cattle Feeders Association
- Texas Chemical Association
- Texas Automobile Dealers Association
- Texas Independent Producers and Royalty Owners Assoc.
- Texas Mid-Continent Oil and Gas Assoc. (now Texas Oil & Gas Association.)
- Texas Natural Gas Pipeline Association

All told, over 472 Bush campaign contributors have been linked to these industries, including 402 individuals and 70 political action committees. Collectively, these representatives gave more than $4 million in contributions to Bush's two gubernatorial campaigns. Since, the figure only includes contributions in excess of $1,000, the 4 million is, almost certainly, at the low end of what may well have gone into the governor's coffers from these interests.

**Donations to Bush Attributable to Various Industries that Lobbied for Audit Privilege Legislation:**

| Business Association | $ to Bush |
|---|---|
| Texas Oil & Gas Assn. | $1,394,204 |
| Texas Chemical Council | $589,200 |
| Texas Assn. of Business & Chambers of Commerce | $567,750 |
| American Electronics Assn. | $483,623 |
| Texas Automobile Dealers Assn. | $467,700 |
| Companies which submitted audits | $274,000 |
| Assn. of Electric Companies of Texas (represents investor-owned utilities) | $215,250 |
| Texas & Southwest Cattle Feeders Assn. | $26,000 |
| **TOTAL** | **$4,017,727** |

- Among these 472 donors were some of the largest donors to Bush's campaigns for governor. No fewer than 86 of these contributors gave $10,000 or more to Governor Bush.

- Seven of the 23 individual donors who gave $100,000 or more to Bush's gubernatorial campaigns were directly affiliated with industry groups that lobbied for the polluter immunity law.

- Seven couples, where the husbands were in key roles at companies which had direct ties to these lobbying groups, personally gave a combined total in excess of $800,000 to Governor Bush's 1994 and 1998 campaigns.

### Contributions to Governor Bush's 1994 and 1998
### Gubernatorial Campaigns

| Individual | Company | Type of Interest | $ to. Bush |
|---|---|---|---|
| M/M Louis Beecherl | Beecherl Investments | Tx Oil & Gas PAC donors | $146,000 |
| Kenneth & Linda Lay | Enron Corp. | TxChemical Council | $122,500 |
| M/M Peter O'Donnell | Tx Oil & Gas | O'Donnell Invest. PAC donors | $118,500 |
| M/M Charles Wyly | Sterling Software | American Electronics Assn. | $111,773 |
| M/M Ray Hunt | HuntOil Co. | Tx Oil & Gas Assn. | $105,000 |
| M/M A. Sanchez | SanchezO'Brien Tx Oil & Gas | Oil & Gas Assn | $101,000 |
| M/M William | McMinn Sterling Grp. | Tx Oil & Gas Assn. | $100,000 |

Additionally, 70 "PACs" which supported both Bush and audit privilege interests were included in the list of the Governor's most generous PAC contributors. Three PACs actually gave Bush in excess of $100,000 toward his campaigns for governor. All three belong to industry associations that supported Texas' polluter immunity legislation:

### PAC Contributions of over $100,000:
### to Bush' 1994 and 1998 Gubernatorial Campaigns

| Political Action Committee | Role in Audit Privilege Lobbying | $ to Bush |
|---|---|---|
| Farmers Employee and Agent PAC | Donor to Business & Commerce PAC | $121,000 |
| Texas Automobile Dealers & Assn. PAC | Texas Automobile Dealers Assn. lobbied for  audit privilege | $114,500 |
| International Bank of Commerce/IBC PAC | Donor to Business & Commerce PAC | $106,000 |

**Thirty-six percent of the Bush donations from audit privilege interests, or $1,452,273, came from just 11 PACs or companies.**

| Company/Association | Business Interest | $ to Bush |
|---|---|---|
| Enron | Tx Chemical Council | $301,500 |
| Sterling Software | American Electronics Assn. | $212,273 |
| Beecherl Investments | Tx Oil & Gas Assn. | $146,000 |
| Farmers Insurance | Tx Assn. of Business and Chambers of Commerce | $121,000 |
| O'Donnell Investments | Tx Oil & Gas Assn. | $118,200 |
| Sanchez O'Brien Oil & Gas Corp | Tx Oil & Gas Assn | $115,000 |
| Tx Automobile Dealers Assn | Tx. Automobile Dealers Assn | $114,500 |
| Wagner & Brown | Tx Oil & Gas Assn. | $112,500 |
| International Bank of Commerce | Tx Assn. of Business & Chamber of Commerce | $106,000 |
| Hunt Oil | Tx. Oil & Gas Assn | $105,000 |
| Sterling Group | Tx. Oil & Gas Assn. | $100,000 |
| **TOTAL** | | **$1,452,273** |

State records show that companies affiliated with Governor Bush's contributors, as a group, utilized the law's immunity provisions far more frequently than did non-contributing Texas companies.

On 246 occasions, Texas companies disclosed an average of four or more violations of Texas environmental laws for which they requested immunity. Companies affiliated with Bush contributors filed only 17 percent of all privileged audits. By comparison, that same group reported 48 percent of all requests for immunity for violations of environmental laws.

| Company | $ to Bush for Governor 1993-98 | Numbers of Audits | Number Privileged Disclosures of Violation |
|---|---|---|---|
| Air Products Inc. | $1,000 | 2 | 1 |
| ALCOA | $1,000 | 2 | 1 |
| American Airlines | $19,500 | 1 | 1 |
| ARCO | $27,500 | 63 | 33 |
| ASARCO, Inc | $1,000 | 9 | 9 |
| Aviall, Inc. Texas | $1,000 | 3 | 0 |
| Bell Helicopter/ Textron | $25,000 | 10 | 4 |
| Burlington Northern | $6,000 | 43 | 1 |
| Central & Southwest Corp | $27,000 | 60 | 1 |
| Champion International Corp | $4,500 | 4 | 2 |
| Chemical Lime Co | $4,000 | 2 | 2 |
| Chevron | $4,000 | 4 | 2 |
| Coastal | $30,000 | 7 | 0 |
| Compaq | $17,000 | 7 | 2 |
| Crown Central Petroleum | $4,000 | 1 | 0 |
| Dow Chemical | $30,000 | 1 | 0 |
| Eastman Chemical Co. | $7,500 | 6 | 0 |
| Crown Central Petroleum | $4,000 | 1 | 0 |
| Dow Chemical | $30,000 | 1 | 0 |
| Eastman Chemical Co. | $7,500 | 6 | 0 |
| Enron | $301,500 | 5 | 1 |
| Exxon | $14,000 | 18 | 0 |
| FINA Inc. | $9,000 | 2 | 0 |
| General Electric | $2,000 | 9 | 3 |
| General Motors | $7,000 | 5 | 2 |
| Greenhill Petroleum Corp. | $4,000 | 4 | 0 |
| Huntsman Corp | $5,000 | 47 | 4 |
| Koch Industries | $34,000 | 1 | 0 |
| Lockheed Martin | $20,000 | 1 | 1 |
| Louisiana Pacific Corp. | $2,000 | 17 | 10 |
| Lyondell Petrochemical | $3,500 | 15 | 2 |
| Marathon Oil Company | $4,000 | 1 | 0 |
| Monsanto/Solutia | $1,000 | 58 | 0 |
| Northcutt Woodwork | $5,000 | 3 | 0 |

| Company | $ to Bush for Governor 1993-98 | Numbers of Audits | Number Privileged Disclosures of Violation |
|---|---|---|---|
| Norton & Co | $1,000 | 1 | 1 |
| Occidental | $21,000 | 29 | 3 |
| Owens Corning | $36,500 | 6 | 3 |
| Phillips Petroleum | $23,000 | 47 | 0 |
| Shell Oil | $42,700 | 7 | 1 |
| Sterling Chemical | $87,000 | 7 | 2 |
| Structural Metals Inc | $11,500 | 1 | 0 |
| Texas Instruments | $35,500 | 9 | 0 |
| Ultramar Diamond Shamrock | $7,500 | 7 | 4 |
| Union Carbide | $3,500 | 15 | 2 |
| Union Carbide | $3,500 | 15 | 2 |
| Union Pacific Resources | $13,000 | 9 | 6 |
| Valero Energy | $32,500 | 11 | 0 |
| Vastar | $1,000 | 12 | 0 |
| **TOTAL** | **$942,700** | **578** | **118** |

Sources: The political donations were made by association and company Political Action Committees, or by employees of member companies in the associations. This total also includes contributions from 22 company PACs (and employees of those companies) that submitted audits but were not linked to the groups that lobbied for the legislation. However, this study *did not* tally donations from individuals who gave less than $1,000 to Bush's gubernatorial campaigns. There are many other contributors who work in the industries on the list but who could not be linked to the associations which advocated for the legislation. Therefore, the totals are minimum amounts.

The total number of violations comes from the TNRCC Environmental Audit Log, 10-29-99. An average of 4.3 violations per date of disclosure comes from statistics given by TNRCC Chairman Barry McBee to the U.S. Senate Committee on the Environment and Public Works, 10-30-97. Source of information

on audits and disclosures by company: TNRCC Environmental
Audit Log, 10-1-99. The analysis of Bush contributors was
performed by PEER and Public Research Works.

In other words, the companies that funded
Governor Bush's campaigns and backed Texas' audit
privilege were more frequently some of the worst polluters
in the state. Thanks to Governor Bush's efforts, they also
reaped the benefit of the immunity privilege law on a
disproportionately higher basis.

# George W. Bush
## *Weakening Environmental Enforcement*

Environmental laws and regulations mean little if they are not enforced. Weak enforcement sends the wrong message to pollution violators—just as it does when it applies to drunk drivers, thieves and other lawbreakers. Weak enforcement occurs not only when regulatory agencies aren't given sufficient resources (funding) to do their job, but also when political appointees running the agency don't want to see the laws and regulations aggressively enforced. Their attitude towards enforcement reflects the attitude of the Governor who appointed them.

The Texas Natural Resource Conservation Commission (TNRCC) has long held the reputation of being a "toothless tiger." While all Texas Governors have talked about vigorous enforcement of environmental laws, there is little evidence over the last decade to suggest that any governor has encouraged enforcement. In fact, the actions of Governor Bush have served to *discourage* enforcement. Under Governor Bush, the "toothless tiger" lacks not only teeth, but also an appetite.

## Cutting the Budget

In 1995 the State Appropriation bill called for a 10 percent cut in the budget of all state agencies, except for the TNRCC. Unfortunately, the bill singled the state environmental agency for a 20 percent cut.[134] This caused Texas to take a free fall, from 16th to 37th nationally, in the percentage of environmental spending allocated in the state budget[135]

The budget cut resulted in fewer numbers of routine inspections of facilities suspected of polluting the environment. Also, by eliminating overtime, the agency's ability to have its inspectors respond to citizen complaints was greatly reduced.[136]

## Inadequate Investigation of Citizen Complaints

When black smoke and noxious odors poured from the Huntsman chemical plant in Odessa, Texas for weeks in early 1999, a local preacher gathered 3100 affidavits from irate community members. They attributed health problems, loss of sleep, and other effects to the pollution that filled the air. However, the 3100 affidavits were not registered in the environmental agency's database of citizen complaints. Residents were so angered by the lack of response by Governor Bush's appointees, that they drove hundreds of miles to the Capitol and held a demonstration in front of the Governor's mansion.

When five residents living near a Southwestern Gas Pipeline facility in Grimes County continued to complain of odors and health effects, they were told by the state environmental agency that it "will no longer investigate your complaints."[137] Even though the facility had a history of problems, the agency claimed previous investigations had not verified the citizens' allegations. However, the agency's "investigations," as is too often the case, usually involved a phone call to the company or a visit which took place many hours after the complaint was made. John Young, the Texas Natural Resource Commission official who made the decision "not to respond" to the citizens complaints, also issued an internal memo which ended the agency's policy of occasional surprise inspections at regulated facilities.

Examples like these, cast doubt on the claims of Governor Bush's appointees who say the number of pollution complaints in Texas are down because people have less to complain about. Instead, many people just give up and stop complaining because it doesn't get the problem solved. Citizens say the agency doesn't document what it chooses to ignore. And, it can't find what it doesn't look for. In both the cases mentioned above, citizens turned to the courts for help.

The Texas environmental agency has long been accused of failing to investigate, or properly investigate, many of the complaints it receives. Public Research Works conducted a comprehensive study of 35,000 complaints logged by the state environmental agency from 1996 through 1999. The report by Public Research Works, "The TNRCC Complaint Process: Is Anybody Listening?" found that health complaints are not often given priority ranking for prompt attention. More than 53% of health complaints received a ranking that required an investigation within 30 days, when resources allowed or none at all. The report also found three quarters of the people, who filed complaints, never received a final letter from the agency letting them know what happened with the investigation. In cases where the agency detects a pollution violation, 58% of the people were never sent a final letter. Public Research Works found evidence of the agency not logging complaints and even telling people not to complain. When citizens call the agency with a pollution complaint, they are sometimes told to call the company causing the problem. After awhile, many people quit complaining because it doesn't do any good.

## Undermine Inspections

An estimated 1,585 industrial facilities in Texas are ranked as major sources of air pollution. There are 75 (minor) sources subject to annual inspection. Field investigators, who work in the sixteen regional offices, perform the annual routine inspections as part of an agreement with the EPA. For approximately twenty-three years, agency inspectors conducted "surprise" annual inspections of Texas' industrial plants (without first calling ahead to inform plant officials they were coming). This allowed inspectors to get an accurate picture of day to day plant operations under "normal" conditions.

On September, 11, 1995, only ten days after the third and final Bush appointee to the TNRCC was announced, the acting division director for Field Operations, John Young, issued a memorandum eliminating "surprise" annual inspections. He mandated that, for all TNRCC programs, site visits be announced with as much as a two-week advance notice. This also included yearly compliance reviews and visible emissions observations of the plant.

The memo stated, "Effective the date of this IOM (inter-office memorandum) it will be the policy of Field Operations Division to provide notification to facilities of our intent to conduct a compliance inspection prior to all-routine inspections. Ideally this notification should occur one to two weeks prior to the inspection date."

In September of 1996, the TNRCC announced that voluntary compliance, rather than mandatory enforcement options, would be the preferred enforcement strategy for its efforts to bring violating facilities into compliance with state law. Although TNRCC chairman Barry McBee issued a press release in late September, 1996, designed to build public confidence in this new policy, the Texas Center for Policy Studies analysis of McBee's statements found them to be seriously misleading. McBee proclaimed that the agency had posted "record enforcement numbers" for fiscal year 1996, that the year "has been the most impressive year in the history of environmental protection in Texas," and that the TNRCC had doubled the fines levied in 1994 and 1995.

In fact, TNRCC's own enforcement records did show that more administrative penalties were imposed in the areas of air quality and petroleum storage tanks in 1996. However, records also showed, and McBee declined to mention, that enforcement in four other areas had decreased dramatically since 1994. These areas were water quality, industrial/hazardous waste, municipal solid waste and agricultural programs.[138]

The study also revealed that the TNRCC was routinely allowing polluters to escape fines through the company's use of Supplemental Environmental Projects (SEPs). The program was originally designed as a method to take money owed to the state as fines and instead, to spend it on a special "Project" that directly benefited the community where the violation had occurred. For a project to qualify, it must "reduce the amounts of pollutants reaching the environment, enhance the quality of the environment, or contribute to the public awareness of environmental matters."[139] Companies who conducted these environmental programs could receive as much as a fifty-percent reduction in administrative fines and penalties.

The TNRCC describes these Supplemental Environmental Projects as a way to "turn money from fines into projects which benefit the community affected by the environmental violations." However, all too often, it was the violating company who actually benefited from reduced fines with little or no corresponding benefit to the community that had been harmed. As earlier examples illustrate, this practice itself preceded Governor Bush's administration; however, since the Governor has been in office, the opportunity for misdirecting penalties has reached new heights.[140]

The Texas Center for Policy Studies carefully scrutinized Supplemental Environmental Projects conducted in 1996 under Bush's administration and found that the agency allowed polluters to use these programs as a way to renovate their own facilities. Approximately 80 percent of the total penalty value of all the Supplemental Environmental Projects in fiscal year 1996 resulted from enforcement actions against just two companies, Diamond Shamrock and Asarco.

In 1996, after both of these companies were found to have committed serious violations of environmental laws, money that would have gone toward fines was allowed to be spent by the companies on supplemental "Projects." The benefit to the community affected by the violation, as opposed to the facility that had violated the law, was questionable at best.

Diamond Shamrock's "Project" primarily involved its replacement of below ground piping with above ground piping within its own facility. Asarco's "Project" primarily involved the removal of an unused Zinc Furnace, also located on its site. Both of these "Projects" represented improvements at the companies' facilities. The cost of these improvements was simply passed over to the public.

## Contributors Benefit from Program Avoid Fines

Between 1996 and 1998 companies that escaped fines through the use of the Supplemental Environmental Programs (SEPs) contributed $116,461 to Bush's gubernatorial campaigns.

| SEP Company | $ to Bush |
|---|---|
| Asarco | $1,000 |
| Champion International Corp | $ 4,500 |
| Dow Chemical Company | $30,000 |
| Fina Oil & Chemical Company | $9,000 |
| Jobe Concrete | $1,000 |
| Occidental | $21,000 |
| Phillips 66 Company | $21,111 |
| Texas Industries | $15,600 |
| Ultramar Diamond Shamrock | $13,250 |
| **TOTAL** | **$116,461** |

Source: Texas Public Employees for
Environmental Responsibility)

# Superfund Toxic Waste Sites
## *A Super Deal for Texas Polluters*

In one of Governor Bush's earliest "environmental" initiatives, he commissioned an industry- dominated group to rewrite Texas' hazardous waste cleanup laws. The Texas Superfund law was designed so as to hold individuals and businesses accountable when their toxic pollution threatens public health. Under Bush, the Texas Superfund law was rewritten, shifting the responsibility for toxic cleanup costs from the banks and landowners to the state taxpayers

The State Superfund program was named after its federal counterpart, which had originally established a large or super *"fund"* to pay for cleanup of abandoned toxic waste sites. The Texas program was created to address those sites (within Texas), that are not ranked high enough to be listed under federal Superfund program, but still were a threat to the environment.

After Bush first took office, the 1997 Texas legislature overhauled the Texas Superfund program when it passed House Bill 2776.[141] Governor Bush signed the legislation putting greater responsibility on Texas taxpayers to pick up the tab for hazardous waste clean up costs by eliminating most of the "polluter pays" principles which were the heart of federal and state hazardous waste cleanup laws. The revised law also limited the citizens' right to know specifics about cleanup matters and deprived them of their ability to ensure that sites located in their communities are left clean.

Beginning in 1993, when Bush began raising money for his first gubernatorial race, until the end of Bush's second campaign for Governor in 1998, the Political Action Committees (PACs) of the Superfund working group gave the Governor $861,011. Counting contributions from PACs and individuals directly associated with the workgroup participants, the total contributed by interested parties increases to $3,159,715.

## Polluters Write Their Own Hazardous Waste Cleanup Policies

Soon after Bush appointed Barry McBee as Chairman of the Texas Natural Resources Conservation Commission in 1995, the agency established another of Bush's "partnerships" with business. This "workgroup" was to reevaluate the state's hazardous waste cleanup programs.[142] Much like the secret industry workgroup that developed Governor Bush's policy on grandfathered polluters, the Superfund workgroup was dominated by the state's most powerful polluters.

Bush ally State Senator Buster Brown, delegated the entire hazardous waste cleanup legislation to this workgroup. Senator Brown, who would also be instrumental in passing legislation for grandfathered polluters, told fellow Senators that the group included "interested parties involved in all aspects of the program, including industry and environmental representatives."[143] In truth, environmentalists and other public representatives had no meaningful role in developing the Superfund cleanup legislation.

## Public Shutout of Superfund Cleanup Reform

Although three environmentalists were listed among the 38 members of the workgroup, each of the two Sierra Club representatives listed stated that they did not participate after attending one or two meetings.[144] The remaining 32 members (of the 35-member panel) and the true crafter of the legislation and the pre-ordained agenda behind it, were from business associations, large companies, and a few from state agencies. These members included, among others, lobbyists for: the Texas Chemical

Council, the Texas Association of Business and Chambers of Commerce, the National Federation of Independent Business, and the Independent Bankers Association of Texas. Representatives of agribusiness, the insurance lobby, and companies including Dow Chemical, Temple-Inland, Dupont and Union Carbide were also included. As stated, seven employees from state agencies were also listed as workgroup members.

Given the makeup of the working group that was to be largely responsible for the legislation, it is not surprising that it enormously favored polluters and property owners who would otherwise be liable for pollution. The highlights of the revised law include:

- Limited liability for lenders and fiduciaries for hazardous waste cleanup and the impact of pollution on the public.

- Extended immunity from liability for off-site contamination, i.e., for contamination of other people's property, under certain conditions.

- Allows the TNRCC Chairman to remove facilities from the state Superfund list even if a landowner has not requested it.

Changed requirements for de-listing state Superfund facilities: Previously, sites could only be taken off the Superfund list after a public contested case hearing; House Bill 2776 changed that requirement to mandate only a "public meeting" before sites were taken off the list.

Ended TNRCC's practice of filing state liens on state Superfund sites. Under the new policy, TNRCC merely sends the landowner a bill.

Allowed new options to resolve polluter liability, including "covenants not to sue," mixed (i.e., partially public) funding for cleanup projects, and "partial settlements" where the polluter pays less than the full cost of the cleanup.

Created a new class of state-defined "Innocent Property Owners," and authorized TNRCC to issue "certificates of innocence" which absolve the property owner of liability for hazardous waste on their properties.

The passage of House Bill 2776 is yet another example of how, under Governor George W. Bush, Texas industry reduced its own legal liability for its conduct, weakened public participation and reduced penalties and enforcement by state agencies charged with the duty of protecting the public health and our environment.

## Further Limiting Liability for Polluted Property

The legislation signed by Governor Bush was designed to and ultimately did limit liability for both lenders and fiduciaries as it related to polluted property. "Fiduciaries," in this context, are the responsible governing officers of a corporation, partnership, or sole proprietorship who finance the redevelopment of toxic sites. When the Independent Bankers Association of Texas and the Texas Association of Bankers both lobbied to pass this bill, they argued that limiting liability would help the economy by more freely allowing lenders to loan money on polluted property. Also, they would know that they could foreclose on bad debts without fear that they would incur liability for cleaning up repossessed, contaminated property.

Limiting polluter liability overturns decades of legal precedent and hard work. The Superfund program and American tort law recognizes the long-established principle that landowners are responsible for cleaning up the remains of polluting activities, and that they pass that liability on to include future owners who may later purchase or receive the property in any manner. Often, the subsequent purchaser will have some recourse against the seller if the property was sold under a misrepresentation or without legally required disclosures. If the lenders do not want the responsibility, even through a later foreclosure, their remedy is to more carefully examine the value of the collateral before they accept it as security for a loan.

Sites that are contaminated and carry with them the duty of cleanup, should not be given the same economic value (and benefit of resale) as sites that have been handled appropriately under state clean up laws. To do so, in essence, financially "cleans up" an otherwise toxic and dangerous piece of property, to the detriment of other competing real estate holders trying to market clean property at a competitive price. By failing to insist on clean up before resale, it also threatens the public at large who will continue to be exposed to the effects of the contamination. Again, the best interest of the public health and safety bows to the interest of polluter profit.

When a polluter is unavailable or unable to pay for cleaning up a contaminated site, the cost of the cleanup falls to the state or federal government. That cost is often quite substantial. Texas' state Superfund program will cost $60 million this biennium alone.[145] Prior to HB 2776, the only real way for polluters to dodge paying the cost of required cleanup was by filing bankruptcy. The Texas economic bust of the late 1980s left many vacant polluted industrial sites with no solvent land owner available to pay clean up costs.

Unfortunately, House Bill 2776, that was supported and signed by Governor Bush, created a brand new class of irresponsible fiduciaries and land owners in Texas. This bill dramatically reduced the make of those included within the classes and, therefore, the actual number of "potentially responsible parties" who were available to be held responsible to pay the cost of hazardous waste cleanup on contaminated properties. The smaller the pool of potentially liable parties, the greater the burden on taxpayers. With fewer private pockets, there is an increased likelihood that some of those responsible parties will default, thereby requiring the public to pick up all or part of the tab.

## Privatizing Profit and Socializing Cost.

The re-written Super Fund law also limited landowner liability in other ways. It allowed companies that entered the state's "voluntary" cleanup program to sell their property without conferring liability for cleanup onto the new purchaser. The same provision allowed banks to foreclose on polluted properties without incurring responsibility for cleaning up the pollution on the property it repossessed.

Before the legislation was passed, the state required owners of polluted property to pay for the full cost of the cleanup. With legislation signed by Governor Bush, new loopholes were created which absolve polluters from liability. These loopholes, that are much more favorable to industry and property owners, include: "covenants not to sue," mixed (i.e., partially public) funding for cleanup projects, and "partial settlements" where the polluter pays less than the full cost of the cleanup, passing the remainder on to the state. Never forget, the tax paying citizens are "the state" (for purposes of paying the tab). Therefore, the absorbed cost of cleaning up, previously paid by the private landowners who created the toxic cesspools, is not being paid by some fictitious charity, but comes out of the pockets of the taxpaying public

## Innocence Found

Another limitation on liability encompassed in the legislation is referred to as the "Innocent Property Owners" program. The idea behind the initiative sounded reasonable on the surface: property owners whose land was polluted by somebody else shouldn't be liable for cleaning it up. The bill authorized the TNRCC to issue "certificates of innocence" to applicants if their property was contaminated as a result of a release or migration of contaminants from a source or sources not located on their property. As of October 1999, 69 certificates had been issued under this program.

This provision poses numerous real problems. First, it overturns longstanding Texas law that historically holds all property owners responsible for cleanup of their own property. Existing statutes and theories of common law negligence and trespass already allow the owner of property that has been contaminated by someone else to force the polluter to pay damages. For participants in the Innocent Property Owners program, House Bill 2776 takes the responsibility of cleaning up contaminated property entirely off the property owners. In the long term, this increases the likelihood that taxpayers must ultimately finance the cleanup of these sites, or that no cleanup will take place at all.

Second, while some industrial sites have been rejected in their applications, others have been excused as "innocent owners" who actually have operations that may themselves pollute. The types of companies that have received "certificates of innocence" include a dry-cleaners, a concrete plant, an ink manufacturer and a chemical products firm.

Finally, the vast majority of innocence certificates approved by the TNRCC have been to excuse cleanup requirements for property designated for residential developments, apartment complexes, shopping centers, and retail outlets. These are places where large numbers of adults and *children* are likely to unknowingly come into close and prolonged contact with the contaminated land.

## Limiting Public Input on Hazardous Waste Cleanup

The re-written hazardous waste clean-up law also went a long way toward limiting significant public input into the adequacy of the state's Superfund hazardous waste cleanup process. It allowed the Texas Natural Resource Conservation Commission's Executive Director to remove facilities from the state Superfund list, even if the request came from someone other than the landowner. Moreover, it changed the requirements for de-listing facilities. Previously, sites could only be taken off the Superfund list after a public contested case hearing at which neighbors of the site had the right to inquire into the sufficiency and quality of the cleanup effort.

Opponents to the change argued that limiting contested case hearings could harm the public interests in several ways. The owner of a contaminated site "might seek to have the designation of a property's use changed from "residential" to "light industrial" in an effort to reduce the standards for clean up. The standard for an industrial site is not as stringent as for a residential area. Residents of neighborhoods located near the re designated property may object to their children growing up next to a contaminated site that has only partly been cleaned up. Members of the affected public should have the ability to present their views in a serious forum, such as a contested case hearing, rather than be relegated to simply listening at a public meeting where there is no legally binding consequence.[146] These arguments were ignored and the new language in the legislation watered down the old requirements for a "public hearing." Now the agency must only have "public meeting."

In a move designed to further lower polluters' profiles with the public, the legislation ended the state's longstanding practice of filing state liens (at the local county courthouse) on properties where state funds had to be used to cleanup hazardous waste. Previously, these liens ensured that future property owners were on notice of liability attaching to the property to cover past cleanup costs. The liens also publicized information as to which properties (and property owners) owed the state money for hazardous waste cleanup.

With Governor Bush's signing of the new state Superfund legislation, the TNRCC now merely sends the owners a written bill in the mail. Copies of these letters are not generally published. Therefore, deadbeat polluters are no longer held publicly accountable for their failure to pay for the state's cleanup of the mess they made in their own backyards.

## Following the Money:
## Contributions from Superfund Working Group

The industries that crafted the plan to overhaul states Superfund hazardous waste cleanup laws donated at least $3.5 million toward George W. Bush's 1994 and 1998 campaigns for Governor. By most analyses, the investments were worth far more than the cost. Once George W. Bush was elected Governor, industry was finally able to get legislation signed that jerked the teeth out of the state Superfund law.

From December 1995 through August 1996, representatives of powerful industry met in a workgroup to hammer out changes in the Superfund law. The Political Action Committees (PACs) of the industry groups represented on this working committee had already donated $386,400 to Bush's two campaigns for governor. The money began pouring in during 1993 and continued through August 1996, when the group concluded its rewrite of the State's Superfund law.

By the time the legislation was drafted and the proposed changes signed into law (in mid-1997) the PACs of the Superfund workgroup had donated an additional $116,000. By 1998, the end of Bush's second gubernatorial campaign, these PACs had donated an additional $358,611. In total, these particular PACs contributed $861,011 to the Governor's campaigns.

### PAC Contributions to George W. Bush Gubernatorial Campaigns from Superfund Workgroup Participants

| Workgroup Participants | Companies & Assns. Represented | 1993-8/96 | 9/96 - 6/97 | 6/97-12/98 | Total |
|---|---|---|---|---|---|
| Ronn Cobb | American Insurance Assn. | $3,000 | $1,500 | $1,000 | $5,500 |
| Allen Beinke | Arter & Hadden | $10,000 | $ - | $10,000 | $20,000 |
| Pam Giblin & Mark J. White | Baker & Botts | $40,000 | $ - | $35,000 | $75,000 |
| Lisa K. Anderson | Brown, McCarroll & Oaks Hartline | $15,000 | $5,000 | $15,000 | $35,000 |
| Sandy Henderson | Dow Chemical Company | $10,000 | $5,000 | $11,000 | $26,000 |
| Jim Kennedy | Dupont | $ - | $ - | $ 1,000 | $1,000 |
| Karen Neeley* | Ind. Bankers Assn.* | $1,000 | $1,000 | $5,000 | $7,000 |
| Lisa Shelton | Motorola | $1,000 | $ - | $4,500 | $5,500 |
| Leonard Dougal & Kathy Hutto | Small, Craig & Werkenthin | $ 500 | $1,000 | $ - | $1,500 |
| Paul Hugon | Temple Inland Forest Products | $10,000 | $5,000 | $10,000 | $25,000 |
| Christopher Shields | Tx Ag Aviation Associates | $ - | $1,000 | $1,000 | $2,000 |
| Mary Miksa | Tx Assn. Bus &Chambers of Comm. | $160,000 | $71,000 | $122,500 | $353,500 |
| Jon Fisher & Mark Shilling | Tx Chemical Council | $66,500 | $13,500 | $61,111 | $141,111 |
| Bill Powers | Tx Farm Bureau | $45,400 | $5,000 | $50,000 | $95,400 |
| Cindy Morphew | Tx Oil & Gas Assn. | $2,500 | $ - | $18,500 | $21,000 |
| Robert E. O'Bryan | Union Carbide Corp | $1,000 | $1,000 | $1,500 | $3,500 |

| Mary Reagan | Winstead, Sechrest &Minick | $20,500 | $6,000 | $11,500 | $38,000 |
| TOTALS | | **$386,400** | **$116,000** | **$358,611** | **$861,011** |

*Karen Neeley, with Independent Bankers Association, also lobbied on behalf of the legislation; however, she was not a member of the workgroup.

PAC contributions tell only a small part of the story. Many company executives and lobbyists, also associated with these interests, have been major contributors to George Bush's gubernatorial campaigns. Many of these individuals not only gave to their company PACs, but also gave directly to candidates from their personal pocketbooks.

When the monies received directly from interested individuals working with these companies are combined with the cash received from PACs associated with the workgroup participants the total contributions sky-rocket to **$3,159,715.**

### PAC & Individual Contributions to George W. Bush Gubernatorial Campaigns from Superfund Workgroup Members

| Company/Association Represented | Total to George W. Bush 1993-98 |
| --- | --- |
| American Insurance Assn. | $24,500 |
| Arter & Hadden | $179,200 |
| Assn. of Fire & Casualty Co | $43,300 |
| Baker & Botts | $76,000 |
| Brown, McCarroll & Oaks Hartline | $35,000 |
| Capital Consultants | $10,750 |
| Dow Chemical Company | $35,100 |
| Dupont | $1,000 |
| Independent Bankers Assn.* | $7,000 |
| Motorola | $5,500 |

| Company/Association Represented | Total to George W. Bush 1993-98 |
|---|---|
| Nat'l Federation of Independent Business | $8,700 |
| Small, Craig & Werkenthin | $1,500 |
| Temple Inland Forest Products | $27,000 |
| Tx Ag Aviation Associates | $9,000 |
| Tx Assn. of Business & Chambers of Commerce | $796,750 |
| Tx Chemical Council | $545,811 |
| Tx Farm Bureau | $100,400 |
| Tx Oil & Gas Assn. | $1,189,204 |
| Union Carbide Corp | $3,500 |
| Winstead, Sechrest & Minick | $38,000 |
| **TOTAL** | **$3,159,715** |

*Lobbied on behalf of the legislation but was not on the workgroup.

### Some of the Most Generous of the Companies Represented on the Workgroup

| Enron | $301,500 | Tx Chemical Council/Tx Oil & Gas Assn. |
|---|---|---|
| Arter & Hadden | $179,200 | Law firm |
| Beecherl Investments | $159,750 | Tx Oil & Gas Assn. |
| Farmers Insurance | $121,000 | Tx Assn. of Business & Chambers of Commerce |
| Sanchez O'Brien Oil & Gas | $115,000 | Tx Oil & Gas Assn. |
| Wagner & Brown | $112,500 | Tx Oil & Gas Assn. |
| International Bank of Commerce | $106,000 | Tx Assn. of Business & Chambers of Commerce |
| Hunt Oil Company | $105,000 | Tx Oil & Gas Assn. |
| The Sterling Group | $100,000 | Tx Oil & Gas Assn./Tx Assn. of Bus. & Cham. of Comm. |

**Some of the Most Generous Individual Contributors
Among the Organizations Represented on the Workgroup**

| Louis Beecherl | $146,000 | Beecherl Investments – oil & gas |
|---|---|---|
| Tom Loeffler | $141,000 | Arter & Hadden |
| Edith & Peter O'Donnell Jr | $141,000 | oil & gas |
| Kenneth & Linda Lay | $122,500 | Enron |
| A. Sanchez | $106,000 | Sanchez O'Brien Oil & Gas Corporation |
| Ray Hunt | $105,000 | Hunt Oil Company |
| William McMinn | $100,000 | Sterling |

Of the companies and individuals who were listed as applicants for the new designation of "Innocent Property Owners,"17 of these companies were directly associated with PACs or individuals who made donations to George Bush's presidential campaign. These companies were represented on the Working Group and gave a total of $384,600.

| Innocent Owner Applicant | $ to Bush 1993-1998 |
|---|---|
| Autozone | $1,500 |
| Centex Corporation | $5,000 |
| Century 21 | $10,000 |
| Chevron* | $3,000 |
| Coastal Products & Chemicals* | $27,000 |
| Ford Motor Company | $12,000 |
| HEB Grocery | $55,000 |
| Home Depot | $2,000 |
| Julius Schepps | $12,400 |
| Norwest Bank | $19,500 |
| Patriot American Hospitality | $20,000 |
| Spec's Liquor | $5,200 |
| Trinity Industries | $22,000 |
| Union Pacific Companies | $42,000 |
| Vinson & Elkins | $133,000 |
| Wells Fargo | $14,000 |
| **TOTAL** | **$383,600** |

# Home on the Range
## *For the Nation's Largest Sewage Dump*

Although Texas is well known for leading the nation in certain kinds of pollution, few people know that Texas is the resting place for hundreds of thousand of *tons* of New York City sewage sludge, and is home to the nation's and the world's largest sewage sludge dump. The 100,000-acre dumpsite is located near the small town of Sierra Blanca, in West Texas.

Although this controversial practice began under the administration of previous governor Ann Richards, Governor George W. Bush's regulatory appointees and staffers have ignored local health concerns and charges of illegal dumping, and actually supported *tripling* the amount of New York's sewage sludge being dumped in Texas. Because "local control" and "property rights" were denied to the citizens in Sierra Blanca, Texas is literally serving as the "pay toilet" for New York City.

## The Recipe for Sewer Sludge

Sewage sludge is produced after human, residential and industrial wastes are combined in wastewater treatment plants. The Environmental Protection Agency's Toxic Release Inventory reveals that millions of pounds of chemicals are discharged to sewage treatment plants across the nation. Over 60,000 toxic substances and chemical compounds can be found in sewage sludge.[147] The sludge can contain petroleum hydrocarbons, heavy metals such as arsenic, chromium, mercury, lead and even radioactive waste products. In addition to cancer-causing chemicals like PCBs, pesticides and pathogens are found in sewage sludge. These include viruses and bacteria such as E. Coli, Salmonella, and Tuberculosis.

## How New York Sewage Came to Rot in Texas

New York City dumped millions of tons of its sewage into the ocean until Congress banned ocean dumping of sewage sludge in 1988. New York's sludge was too contaminated with toxic pollutants for any commercial use and too expensive to be buried safely in landfills. In fact, the waste was so bad that New York state law prohibited the sludge from being spread or even landfilled in New York.[148] Apparently, what was too bad for New York was good enough for Texas. In 1992, New York City awarded Merco Joint Venture, an Oklahoma-based company with alleged tied to organized crime, a six-year contract worth $168 million, to dispose of nearly a fifth of the Big Apple's sewage sludge.[149]

Oklahoma was the first place Merco tried to dump the sludge. However, citizen protests, mostly by farmers and ranchers, stopped Merco at five different places they targeted for sludge dumping. A resolution passed by the Oklahoma Senate effectively prevented Merco from dumping in Oklahoma. Since Merco was under a contract deadline to begin dumping New York City's sewage sludge as soon as possible, they turned their sites toward Texas. Texas politicians and regulators, who were less concerned about the environment, could be dealt with. Merco targeted Hudspeth County and a quiet little town called Sierra Blanca, located more than 2,000 miles from New York and the source of the contamination.

Merco had several hurdles to overcome before it could begin dumping on Texas. First there were regulations which prevented sewage sludge from a state with stronger sludge standards from being dumped in a state with weaker standards. Texas was the host-state with the *weaker* standards. This problem was solved for Merco when Texas regulators simply ignored the regulations.[150] Merco also needed a "sludge registration" from the Texas regulators, which normally took many months to obtain.

This problem was easily solved, by greasing the skids of the "registration" process with money.

Merco donated $1.5 million dollars to Texas Tech University to "study" the "beneficial" uses of sludge. Then, quietly, without ever obtaining an environmental impact statement, or utilizing the public process to allow public hearings and an opportunity for questions, Merco was given a 6-year "beneficial land use" sludge registration. The approval came from the environmental agency appointees of Governor, Ann Richards. Merco was granted the 6-year sludge registration in an unprecedented 23 days.[151] It probably didn't hurt that Merco's Project Director, James Johnson, gave $11,000 to Ann Richards' gubernatorial campaign.[152]

What was too bad for New York and Oklahoma was apparently just fine for Texas. Merco began hauling 255 tons of sludge a day from New York and dumped it at Merco's Sierra Blanca "ranch." The sludge was to be spread on 78,500 of the 102,555 acres. According to Environmental Protection Agency employee and sludge critic Hugh Kaufman, "The fish in New York are being protected. The people in New York are being protected. The people in Texas are being poisoned."

## Life Next to the Sludge Dump

In 1992, shortly after dumping began, the people of Sierra Blanca began to complain of the odor. "The chemical odors coming off the application area are not just a nuisance and a trespass, they're a health hazard. Hydrogen sulfide and ammonia vapors mixed with a fecal smell are indescribable - except to say that it smells like death," said local resident and community leader Bill Addington. After citizens complained, "The Texas Air Control Board came down two days later and told us it was just cow patties."[153]

But the odor wasn't the only problem. " We noticed strange rashes and blisters in the mouth, more flu, more colds, more allergies, and asthma since they came. We've seen a lot more sickness - especially with the kids," says Addington. The New York flu virus even made the rounds in Van Horn in 1996, a larger town 34 miles to the east. Sam Dodge, a Merco neighbor and rancher tried to sell his ranch to escape the smell, but none would buy it.

In 1993 twenty Sierra Blanca residents went to a state environmental agency conference in El Paso to protest the problems caused by Merco's sludge dumping. According to Sierra Blanca resident Bill Addington, "We were told by agency officials that the odors we were smelling were from Sierra Blanca's waste water treatment plant. Sierra Blanca has no waste water treatment plant."

After years of illness and governmental inaction, citizens in Sierra Blanca filed a formal civil rights complaint with the U.S. Environmental Protection Agency against the Texas Natural Resource Conservation Commission in 1997.

## New York Sludge - A "Triple Threat" Under the Bush

In 1997, during the administration of Governor Bush, Merco applied to the state environmental agency (TNRCC) to renew their sludge "registration" for an additional ten years. The company also asked that it be allowed to *triple* the amount of sewage spread per acre. Merco hired Governor Bush's former legislative director, Cliff Johnson, to lobby the commissioners of the Texas Natural Resource Conservation Commission, all of whom were Bush appointees, for approval of its request. The registration renewal/amendment was designated so as to allow up to 400 *tons* of sludge to be dumped *each day*.

The Bush-appointed Commissioners approved Merco's request without a public hearing. Once the permit was a "done deal," citizens exercised the only recourse they had available. They asked the Commissioners to reconsider their decision. The agency claimed that the Merco operation was not a threat to the community's health or to the environment, and that "Properly digested and stabilized, sludge may have an earthy odor when it is first applied, but the odor will soon disappear."[154] The citizens' request for reconsideration was denied and Merco continued dumping New York's sludge on Texas. Beginning in 1998, Merco's new ten-year contract for disposing of New York City's sewage sludge is worth $450 million.

## Illegal Dumping Charged at Sierra Blanca

Finally, the citizen's allegations were found to be true. In 1999, Merco admitted that it had spread New York sewage sludge that had not been properly treated to reduce pathogens, as required by state and federal law.[155] In fact, Merco had previously been caught (in 1994) spreading untreated sludge at Sierra Blanca. For that violation, it was fined $12,800. As with too many TNRCC fines, the amount apparently was not enough to deter future violations, especially given the amount of profits involved. Instead of suspending its permits or even requiring that the sludge be properly treated before it was shipped from New York to Texas, as is required by law, the TNRCC simply suggested that Merco mix the untreated sludge with lime on site.[156]

Every day, the tons of sewage sludge keep coming to Texas. It comes with the blessing of Governor Bush and his environmental agency appointees who exercise 'control' over the local citizens of Sierra Blanca.

# George W. Bush: Making Texas
## *The Nation's Nuclear Waste Dump Site*

Congress passed legislation in the 1980's that encouraged States to join "regional compacts" to develop dumpsites for low-level radioactive waste. Pressure for the legislation came mainly from the nuclear power industry that needed more places to dump their radioactive waste. The incentive for states to build these dumpsites was big money. If Texas could agree to a "compact" with other states, and develop a disposal site for their waste and its own, Texas would be guaranteed $50 million to cover construction, plus hundreds of millions of dollars in disposal fees.[157]

Under the administration of Texas Governor Ann Richards, an agreement (compact) was negotiated with Maine and Vermont to have their waste sent to Texas.[158] Incredibly, state officials looked to the small town of Sierra Blanca as the dumpsite. Sierra Blanca, near El Paso and the Mexican border, is 70% Hispanic with 40% of the population at the poverty level and was already targeted for the dumping of New York City's sewage sludge.

One of Governor Bush's first federal initiatives was to ensure the passage of legislation to provide the needed funding for the Texas-Maine-Vermont low-level radioactive waste compact. The federal legislation was first initiated by Governor Ann Richards but was defeated in 1995 after citizens groups fought it for three years. Governor Bush made bringing nuclear waste to Texas one of his priorities.

Using taxpayer monies, Governor Bush and his official lobbyist in Washington, D.C. took charge to make certain the federal compact legislation would pass when it was presented the second time around. The so-called "three-state" compact legislation Bush fought for was aimed at bringing waste into Texas from all over the nation, not just from Maine and Vermont.

Over the vigorous objections of local citizens and statewide environmental groups, Governor Bush's appointees to the Texas Natural Resource Conservation Commission (TNRCC) took the first step towards approving the dumpsite by issuing a draft permit to the Texas Low-Level Radioactive Waste Disposal Authority in 1996. The TNRCC claimed the dumpsite would "not pose an unacceptable risk to public health or safety or cause long-term detrimental impact on the environment." The agency's final decision would follow a legal-style "contested case hearing" where citizens groups, with little money for lawyers and experts, would go up against the state agencies and utility company lawyers.

Citizen groups like "Save Sierra Blanca" and the "Sierra Blanca Legal Defense Fund" pointed out that there was a history of earthquakes in the region and a fault existed directly beneath the site where the waste was to be dumped.[159] However, the state environmental agency characterized the earthquake fault as a mere "bedrock anomaly" and dismissed the citizens' concerns as unfounded.

According to opponents, the Sierra Blanca site had a host of problems. The "low-level" radioactive waste contains elements like plutonium, some of which remain radioactive for hundreds of thousands to even millions of years. If Governor Bush and his agency appointees had their way, these wastes would be buried over an underground fault posing the possibility of earthquakes. Furthermore, the dump was to be built over a groundwater aquifer, only five miles from the town of Sierra Blanca and 16 miles from the Rio Grande River.

## The Nation's Trash Can for Radioactive Garbage?

While the citizens were fighting the state's effort to grant a permit for the Sierra Blanca dumpsite, Governor George W. Bush's team of lobbyists worked the US Congress on an almost daily basis for two years to ensure federal funding would be available to build the dump. Governor Bush and his lobbyists were also trying to make sure that the Texas dump would be able to service the nuclear power industry, not only in the three compact states, but nation-wide.

In November 1996, Roy Coffee, head of the Austin Office of State-Federal Relations, became the Coordinator for Texas' lobbying strategy on the compact legislation. At the direction of the Governor's office, the Texas lobbying agency officially joined the Compact Coalition, a Washington, DC-based group of nuclear utility lobbyists and lobbyists for the states of Maine and Vermont.[160] Weekly reports from lobbyists involved in meetings with representatives of the Governor's office and others establish a pattern of lobbying coordination that continued unabated up until September of 1998. In time, Bush's lobbying efforts, which were funded by Texas taxpayers, would pay off.

## Double Talk and Misrepresentations

Supporters of the radioactive waste dump often said most of the waste would be "medical," like booties, gloves, and other materials associated with hospital X-ray rooms. In reality, the primary constituent (more than 90%) of "low-level" radioactive waste was going to be nuclear reactor waste from nuclear power plants.[161] While Bush campaigned in West Texas for his second term as Governor, he was plagued with questions about the proposed radioactive waste site. In response, he misrepresented the nature of the waste he wanted brought to Texas. In early 1998 he told the Associated Press that the Sierra Blanca site was the solution to a (supposed) low-level radioactive waste "crisis" in El Paso. Bush said there "were tons of X-rays piled up in the El Paso hospitals."[162] This was simply not true.

Bush's statement was directly contradicted by Pete Duarte, the CEO of El Paso's local county hospital. Mr. Duarte said, "I am not aware that this is occurring. Nobody has brought to my attention that we have a problem with radioactive waste. If we are creating a problem, I want to know about it. I don't want to dump it on our neighbors. The last place I would want the waste to go would be to Sierra Blanca."[163] Mr. Duarte also made it clear that X-ray film was not radioactive and was not being dumped anywhere. X-ray film was recycled.

In fact, 97% of the waste coming to the Sierra Blanca site would be from nuclear power plants. Medical waste made up less than 1% of state and national waste streams, both in radioactivity and volume. Medical waste comprised .004% of all the nuclear waste disposed of by Texas, Maine and Vermont in the last 5 years.[164]

The obvious question is this: Did Governor Bush really know what kind of waste the legislation he was pushing would bring to Texas? The prospect that he didn't know would *almost* as frightening as the prospect that he really did know and didn't tell the truth. In fact, Bush did know the truth.

Five months before Bush told the people and the news media in El Paso that the radioactive waste would be mostly limited to hospital X-rays and the like, he signed a letter urging Maine to send radioactive waste from its decommissioned nuclear power plant to Texas.[165]

Despite mounting opposition to the dumpsite from within Texas, Bush's national lobby effort moved forward. Bush's plan for a national-class dumpsite ran into trouble when Texas Congressman Lloyd Doggett amended the federal legislation to ensure that waste from outside of Texas could only come from Maine and Vermont, and nowhere else. The Doggett amendment passed by 3/4 of the US House of Representatives and by all of the US Senate in early 1998. The legislation, restricting the source of the waste to Texas, Maine and Vermont, was then sent to a joint House-Senate conference committee to come up with a compromise on details.

In a move that ensured waste could flood into Texas from every state across the country, Governor Bush lobbied the conference committee and asked its members to remove the Doggett amendment. Bush's lobbying effort ran contrary to longstanding congressional protocol by which small conference committees do not change language agreed upon by both the House and the Senate.

In an April 1998 letter from Governor Office to Rep. Thomas Bliley, the Chairman of the House Committee Governor Bush wrote:

> "...we are writing to you as Chairman of the House Commerce Committee to express our concerns regarding the amendments to H.R. 629, the Texas-Maine-Vermont compact...Our primary concern is the effect these amendments will have on the compact...Our secondary concern is the infringement on state sovereignty if the conference committee accepts these amendments...We urge you to support removal of these amendments in the conference committee and to support quick passage of the Texas-Maine-Vermont compact..."

The irony of Bush's position was his use of the old "state's rights" argument to make sure Texas state government could bring in radioactive waste over the objections of local governments opposed to the dump. Bush's position certainly contradicted his professed beliefs about the need for more "local control." Furthermore, Bush used federal laws and regulations, which he now calls "heavy-handed," to take local control away from local governments.

At the same time Governor Bush was lobbying Congress, officials in Mexico were organizing to oppose the dump. The Mexican National Chamber of Deputies and Senate unanimously passed a resolution against the Sierra Blanca dump in April of 1998. The resolution called for a commission of legislators to meet with Governor Bush to convey their strong opposition. The resolution also voiced the belief that the proposed dump violated the spirit of the commitments embodied the La Paz Agreement. The La Paz Agreement, which was signed by President Ronald Reagan with Mexico in 1985, established a 62-mile zone on each side of the border. It was agreed that there were to be no major projects, by either country, within these environmentally sensitive zones without consultation and input from the other.

Governor Bush continued his lobbying efforts, despite protests by hundreds of Texas citizens and even visits to the nation's capitol by federal Mexican Senators and representatives. Bush and other supporters of the Texas dumpsite suffered a setback when, the week before the vote was to be taken in the US House of Representatives, the nuclear power plant in Maine said it no longer wanted to send its waste to Texas. The company said it wanted out of the compact because it thought it could get its decommissioned nuclear power plant disposed of more quickly and cheaply at another dumpsite.[166]

So desperate was Governor Bush to get the legislation passed, and to get Maine's nuclear waste sent to Texas, he apparently offered Maine a special deal in the last days before the vote. Maine would still pay Texas the $25 million for its share of the dump's construction, but could sell its space in the dump to another state or states. Bush also promised to "pursue as expeditiously as possible the licensing of all disposal shipments, specifically including the disposal of oversize decommissioning components."[167]

Unfortunately for the citizens in southwest Texas and the adjoining Mexican Border area, Bush was successful in his national lobbying efforts. The House Conference Committee stripped away Congressman Dogget's amendment that would have limited the origin of waste coming into Texas. Texas citizen groups were outdone by their Governor and hundreds of thousands of taxpayer and nuclear lobbyist dollars. The legislation that was passed was hardly a "regional" compact as envisioned by the Low-Level Radioactive Waste Policy Act. In June of 1998, the misnamed "Texas-Maine-Vermont compact bill" was passed, and with it, Texas was poised to become the radioactive dumping ground for the entire country. President Bill Clinton signed the legislation into law in September of 1998.

## George W. Bush's Doubletalk Continues

After the compact legislation was passed, all was not right between Texas and Mexico. On June 26, 1998, Governor Bush attended a meeting of Mexican and US Governors in Brownsville, Texas. The press conference was dominated by off-handed questions about the radioactive waste dump. Bush responded with more doubletalk. The El Paso Times wrote: "Bush said he agrees with the spirit of an amendment by U.S. Representative Lloyd Doggett that would restrict the proposed compact to low-level nuclear waste from those three states." However, Bush's words were directly contradicted by his own efforts to strip Rep. Doggett's amendment from the final legislation. Bush was quoted as saying, "If it (the legislation) passes without that amendment, I think it makes sense for the governor to propose a bill out of the Texas Legislature that forever limits low-level radioactive waste to Texas, Maine, and Vermont."

Of course, Governor Bush never asked the legislature to do anything to stop or even limit the radioactive waste from coming to Texas.

## Local Control and States Rights Denied

Governor Bush's effort to bring the radioactive waste to Texas was characterized by his critics as shoving an unwanted waste dump down the throats of Texans. A statewide poll done in November 1994 showed that 82% of Texans counties opposed the use of their state as a nuclear dump.[168] By August 15, 1998, the governments of twenty Texas Counties and 13 Texas cities passed resolutions opposing the radioactive waste dump that Governor Bush had lobbied for behind the scenes. Governor Bush's actions contradicted his claim to believe in "local control."

The federal law that Governor Bush helped to bring about established a bureaucracy that allowed no "local control." Instead, it established a special commission of eight people who would be appointed, not elected. They were to set their own salaries and establish the fees to be charged for the waste that would pour into Texas.[169] Six of the commissioners were to be appointed by the Texas Governor and one each by Maine and Vermont. Because of Bush's lobbying efforts in Washington, the people of Texas would have no say in where the waste came from or the type of waste that would come.

While Governor Bush and his utility company supporters won the fight for federal legislation to fund a Texas dumpsite, they lost the fight for a state permit to put the dump in Sierra Blanca. The coalition of Sierra Blanca residents, environmental groups, and local governments on both sides of the border (including the City and County of El Paso) successfully challenged the permit even though they had little money for lawyers and experts. The utility companies, along with two state agencies, the Texas Low-Level-Radioactive Waste Disposal Authority, (LRWDA), and the Texas Natural Resource Conservation Commission had spent millions of dollars for lawyers and experts to argue for putting the dump in Sierra Blanca. The legislature gave $5.6 million dollars to the state radioactive waste disposal authority to pay for lawyers and experts fighting against 21 environmental groups, local governments and landowners, and individuals who opposed the dump.

In this rare case, well funded, special interests did not prevail against well-organized citizen groups. The administrative law judge found, just as the citizens had claimed from the beginning, that the proposed site was not shown to be suitable for a nuclear waste dump. The judge also expressed concerns that the site may have been chosen because its low income and predominately Hispanic population did not appear to have the resources to oppose the site.

Apparently, the controversy surrounding the radioactive dumpsite was too hot, especially for a politically ambitious Governor. According to political insiders, Bush's popularity ratings among potential Hispanic voters in the El Paso area were declining. In October of 1998, a month before his second run for Governor, Bush's environmental agency appointees voted to accept the administrative law judges recommendation that the permit for the Sierra Blanca dump site, be rejected. The radioactive waste dump that Governor Bush fought to bring to Sierra Blanca would have to wait.

The victory was sweet for some, but somewhat hollow for many others. Because of Governor George W. Bush's successful lobbying efforts at the nation's capitol, Texas remains the designated host for the nation's nuclear waste. Private companies are now scrambling to open new Texas dumps that many people fear will take both commercial nuclear power plant waste, and wastes generated by federal nuclear weapons plants.

# Keeping Texas the Leader
## *In Hazardous Waste-Burning Cement Plants*

Midlothian is a tiny Texas town located 30 miles north of Dallas. It is known as the cement capitol of the nation because of the cement-making companies in the area. Texas Industries (TXI), one of the largest, has been in the business since 1960. Since the 1980's, TXI has also become one of the nation's largest hazardous waste-burning facilities, because it uses commercial hazardous wastes to fuel its processes.

In the early 1990's TXI began its efforts to renew its state and federal permits to operate. The company wanted permission to almost *triple* the volume of hazardous waste it could burn, from 100,000 tons to 270,000 tons per year. Throughout the 1990's there was growing citizen opposition to TXI's waste-burning practices because of the intolerable pollution it caused for miles downwind.

Before George W. Bush took office in 1995, the Texas Natural Resource Conservation Commission had finally started to respond to citizen concerns about the cement plants, which were functioning as large hazardous waste incinerators. Finally, after years of public pressure, the state environmental agency was aggressively reviewing TXI's proposals to assess the risks to the community caused by its emissions. These "risk assessments," which are required as part of the permitting process, determined how much of a risk a facility's operation creates for nearby communities. The outcome of the assessments was critical in deciding whether or not to approve the company's permit. In 1994 the state agency, run by the appointees of the previous Governor, had sent at least two "notice of deficiency" letters to TXI stating that the company's draft risk assessment documents were flawed or inadequate[170]

Citizens groups opposed TXI's permit, which allowed the use of commercial hazardous waste to fuel the company's processes, and resulted in massive amounts of air pollution from the company's stacks. While local citizens were opposing TXI's permitting, large industrial operations across the state, like refineries and chemical companies, had a vested interest in TXI being given its permit. These industries relied upon TXI's four cement kilns as a cheap way to process and dispose of their hazardous wastes.

## Letting the Fox Guard the Henhouse

In May of 1995, Governor Bush made his first appointment to the TNRCC, the state environmental agency that would directly decide on TXI's pending permit request. He appointed Ralph Marquez, who had previously (in 1994) been employed as a consultant to TXI. Among Marquez's duties had been to help organize citizen tours of TXI's facility in an effort to gain public support for its toxic waste incineration. Marquez was also a former Monsanto Chemical Company executive and had worked for the Texas Chemical Council as Vice President for Environmental Affairs.

The Marquez appointment to the TNRCC, and his support and connection to TXI, was critical for much of Texas' industry. Many of the Texas Chemical Council's member companies sent their hazardous waste to TXI for cheap disposal. As a voting member of the state environmental agency, Marquez was in a position to make sure the company got the permits it needed. Marquez was the ace in the hole for TXI and the Texas' hazardous waste generating industries, the same industries that were also leading contributors to Governor Bush's political campaigns.

## Conflict of Interest Ignored

In November of 1995, the TNRCC presented their final "risk assessment" on TXI's operations at a public hearing. The agency report concluded that the proposed increase in hazardous waste burning (from 100,000 to 270,000 tons per year) posed no health hazard in Midlothian or downwind in the Dallas/ Ft. Worth metroplex. With TNRCC's "risk assessment" determined that there were no risks from TXI's emissions, the stage was set for TXI to receive its permit.

On Earth Day, in April of 1996, Dallas and Midlothian area citizens formally requested that Commissioner Marquez recuse himself from the final vote set on TXI's permit. Marquez had indicated publicly on one occasion that he would abstain from voting on TXI-Midlothian issues because of his apparent conflict of interest.[171]

## Ignoring "Best Science" and Known Risks

Alarmed by the questionable conclusions of TNRCC's risk assessment reports, the environmental organization "Downwinders-at-Risk," together with the American Lung Association commissioned a study to review the TNRCC reports. The evaluation was conducted by two independent public health scientists from the University of Michigan School of Public Health, and concluded that the TNRCC risk assessment of TXI was seriously flawed and had improperly excluded critical factors from its consideration.[172]

The public health scientists also found that the state's "risk assessment " agency had seriously underestimated the risks associated with the transportation, storage, handling, and incineration of hazardous waste, and also failed to adequately address issues of bio-accumulation of toxics and accidental releases of toxics. A total of 29 major errors, omissions, and other public health concerns were identified.[173]

Dr. Stuart Batterman from the University of Michigan School of Public Health, summarized the flaws in the TNRCC analysis with these remarks:

"The Screening Analysis and Summary Report are useful starting points for prioritizing future studies and actions aimed at protecting public health and the environment. However, if viewed as technical support documents to justify TNRCC declarations of no substantial risk to public health due to pollution in Midlothian, they must be criticized due to their many serious omissions, inconsistencies, and inadequate or misleading analyses."[174]

"The omission of many hazardous compounds and the selective use of available emission data among other reasons mean that Screening Analysis has not evaluated or has improperly evaluated some of the potentially largest chemical causes of cancer and non-cancer risks. Additionally, the TNRCC estimated, but omitted from the Screening Analysis, relatively high risk estimates for on-site TXI property which is being used for agricultural purposes."[175]

Dr. Batterman determined that not only were the TNRCC's conclusions seriously flawed, he also found that adverse environmental and health impacts on neighboring citizens were likely to occur given the level of industrial activity in the area.

"Based on risk assessment techniques, other environmental impact assessment methodologies, and an assessment of existing environmental monitoring data, we conclude that environmental and health impacts have and are likely to occur in the Midlothian area"[176]

Perhaps even more alarming was his conclusion that pollution from TXI and other industrial sources in the area was particularly dangerous for children. This conclusion was supported by toxicology expert Dr. Marvin Legator, who conducted a health symptom survey that compared the health problems of Midlothian area residents to a control community in Ellis County. His survey showed that citizens in Midlothian had *three times* the rate of respiratory illness from air pollution.:

"For example, concentrations of arsenic, beryllium, cadmium, chromium and lead in the soil show patterns associated with the major sources, and soil levels appear to be increasing. Further, there is a high likelihood that the environmental and health impacts are significant, as demonstrated by exposures and risks that greatly exceed US EPA target exposure levels for a variety of exposure scenarios and source assumptions at a large number of sites. Exceedances of acceptable risk levels for children at all residential locations, is especially noteworthy. These risk estimates exclude impacts from other industrial facilities in Midlothian, some of which are expected to have greater impacts than the TXI facility."[177]

The TNRCC was also criticized for its tendency to exaggerate safety claims beyond what hard science would support. Dr. Legator concluded his evaluation by questioning whether Bush's TNRCC is seriously committed to protecting public health given their poor history of enforcing existing pollution control laws.

"...the TNRCC must be strongly criticized for its tendency to go far beyond what is scientifically supportable by the existing data in making sweeping generalizations regarding the present and future safety of waste combustion in Midlothian. In any event, statements with little or frail scientific basis show a disregard for the protection of public health, and serve to diminish the TNRCC's credibility with the public."[178]

"Finally, the record is deeply troubling regarding activities by the TNRCC related to inspection and enforcement, and TXI with respect to compliance and responsiveness."[179]

The criticisms of the new Bush packed TNRCC echoed those raised by citizens from around the state who were trying to protect their communities. Time after time, they petitioned the agency for protection only to find the state environmental agency, which was supported with their tax dollars and charged with the duty to protect the State's resources, aligning itself with the polluters. The TNRCC's action on the TXI permit made it clear that the Bush appointees were committed to helping industry minimize its duty to clean up their pollution, even as evidence of harm to the public was mounting.

In August of 1997, the TNRCC again delayed action and failed to adopt adequate ozone pollution cleanup plans for the Dallas-Fort Worth area. Six months later, in February 1998, the EPA announced that the DFW area had surpassed its previous "moderate" air pollution levels and must now be reclassified as "serious." The toxic emissions from TXI, combined with emissions from the Midlothian area, combine to form the largest source of smog-forming ozone pollution in North Texas[180]

The TNRCC chose to ignore the findings of the citizens' experts, and instead granted TXI's permit. Although commissioner Marquez had previously indicated that he might abstain on any vote on the TXI-Midlothian issues because of his apparent conflict of interest, he changed his mind. The Bush-appointed commissioner, a former employee of TXI, voted for TXI's permit.

In March of 1999 a group of citizens from Midlothian went to the State Capitol for a TNRCC hearing and to protest and picket on the sidewalk in front of the Governor's mansion. They brought enough petitions to make a ring along the sidewalk around the mansion. They hoped that these petitions and voices would force the governor to hear and acknowledge the seriousness of their concerns. That was not to be the case. These protestors happened to arrive at the same time that speculation was high on whether George W. Bush planned to run for the office of President of the United States.

Everyone suspected that Governor Bush did not want negative publicity focussing public attention on his true environmental record. However, they were not prepared for what happened. While concerned citizens were peacefully protesting on the public sidewalk, as is the time-honored tradition in Texas, they were approached by Governor Bush's Protective Detail and ordered to leave the public sidewalk under threat of arrest. One protester, a PTA mother who didn't move fast enough, was arrested, handcuffed, and placed in a patrol car. She was released only after others pleaded her case and told the officers that she needed to pick up her children from daycare.

## Following the Money: From TXI to Bush

Texas Industries CEO, Robert Rogers, together with his wife gave $3000 to Bush for his first Gubernatorial Campaign in 1994.. Texas Industries Political Action Committee contributed $2000 to Governor Bush's 1998 gubernatorial campaign.[181]

# "Property Rights" and "Local Control"
## *What they Really Mean to Bush*

Political slogans, much like 'sound bites' and 'one liners,' are composed of carefully chosen words that stir our emotions. Slogans don't require explaining by the politician using them, or much thinking by the person listening. Slogans may be illuminating but rarely are they enlightening. They are used to make us feel and react—not to think and then take action. That's why politicians love to use them, sometimes even to mask and deceive.

Governor Bush has turned several of his campaign slogans into battle cries such as his demand to "Let Texans Run Texas" and his call for more "Local Control" and "Property Rights." These slogans appeal to people because they speak to the frustrating lack of control people have over many aspects of their lives. Many decisions affecting our families and our property, have in fact, been taken from us at the local level.

Three laws which were passed by the Texas legislature during the first year of Gov. Bush's administration show the way catchy slogans can be used to spearhead an otherwise unpopular, often unsupportable, cause. Each law, passed under the banner of Bush's familiar campaign slogans, actually benefited special interest groups who contributed to Bush's campaign and stripped Texas communities of powers to manage growth and protect the environment.

## Stripping Control from the Locals

One of the first acts of the Bush administration in 1995 was to push legislation that would limit the ability of state and local governments to enforce environmental protections like the Endangered Species Act. The legislation was called the Private Real Property Rights Preservation Act (Senate Bill 14), and was part of a national campaign intended to limit environmental protections.

The bill used language in the U.S. Constitution's Fifth Amendment that stated that no government may "take" private property for public use without just compensation. This bill was a radical reinterpretation of constitutional law that greatly expanded the definition of "taking" and argued that environmental regulations "took" private property. The bill allowed governments or their agencies to be sued if an action they took reduced the value of private property by 25 percent or more.

Unfortunately, Governor Bush's concept of "property rights" does not extend to citizens whose property is damaged by big business polluters. The citizens of Sierra Blanca and Midlothian also have "property rights," but they cannot sue the government for recklessly granting permits to industries that pollute their entire communities. Neither can citizens sue the government for taking taxpayers money and then failing to enforce environmental protection. Citizens whose property was severely devalued by polluters were not considered, much less given any right or recourse under Bush's "property rights" agenda. In both cases, the actions of Governor Bush and his appointees have stripped communities and city and county governments of "local control."

Critics of the so-called "Property Rights Act" say it is more accurately described as the "Polluter Protection Act." By associating this legislation with the noble cause of protecting "property rights," much of the public was lulled into accepting laws that force taxpayers to pay corporations or land speculators to comply with environmental laws. The Lone Star Chapter of the Sierra Club characterizes the bill as a means which "will force taxpayers and ratepayers to pay polluters not to pollute."[182]

Marshall Kuykendall, the leader of an organization called "Take Back Texas," was also a leading proponent of the law who said, "the last time the federal government took our property without compensation, is when Lincoln freed the slaves."[183] His statements were made in forums organized to oppose the Endangered Species Act and to build support for "private property rights" legislation.

The Private Real Property Rights Preservation Act was pushed through the legislative process. Demonstrating the importance of the new law to his agenda, Governor Bush traveled to the Texas Farm Bureau Headquarters in Waco to sign the legislation.[184]

## Private Property Rights *for Some*

During Gov. Bush's first legislative session in 1995, The Private Real Property Rights Preservation Act (Senate Bill 14) was promoted by agricultural and business groups to thwart the Endangered Species Act and other environmental initiatives. The groups that supported the bill contributed more than $1.3 million to Governor George W. Bush's gubernatorial campaigns.

### Contributions to Governor Bush from Lobby Groups Supporting SB 14

| | |
|---|---:|
| National Federation of Independent Business | $8,700 |
| Tx & Southwest Cattle Raisers Assn. | $387,100 |
| Tx Assn. of Business & Chambers of Commerce | $795,750 |
| Tx Landowners Council | $1,500 |
| Tx Farm Bureau | $100,500 |
| Tx Wildlife Assn. | $53,209 |
| Other supporters | $3,500 |
| **TOTAL** | **$1,350,279** |

Source: Public Research Works.

These figures include contributions from the PACs, PAC donors, and lobbyists of these associations to the gubernatorial campaign funds of George W. Bush. They do not take into account the funds spent by these groups in their lobbying efforts or contributions to other Texas politicians.

Many of the organizations on the frontline of the private property rights program were business associations and corporate think tank groups (rather than individual companies). Two other groups that appeared to help Governor Bush to "Let Texans Run Texas" were made up of real estate types and landowners, labeling themselves "Take Back Texas," and the "Southwest Texas Property Rights Association."

Another of the many groups lobbying on the legislation was the Texas Landowners Council, represented at the Capitol by Terral Smith. Smith was an early supporter of George W. Bush's gubernatorial ambitions, giving Bush money as early as 1993. Smith was later hired by the Governor to work as his Legislative Director.

Among the major supporters of "property rights" and other anti-environmental legislation was a new group called "Texas Citizens for a Sound Economy." The national parent group of this association, "CSE," was profiled recently in a January, 2000 article in *the Washington Post* entitled, "Think Tanks: Corporations' Quiet Weapon." The *Post* obtained an internal document from CSE, which had "the most precise illustration yet of the close fit between "Texas Citizens for a Sound Economy" funding and corporate interests." Gary Ruskin of the Congressional Accountability Project characterized CSE as "a rent-a-mouthpiece...These are mercenary groups that function as surrogates when industry feels it is not advantageous for it to speak directly."

When the interest of local voters are in conflict with the interests of wealthy politically connected developers, the voters are in big trouble. Voters in Austin learned firsthand that Bush's slogan of "Local Control" has more than one meaning.

Austin, the capitol of Texas, is home to Barton Creek and to the historic area of Barton Springs. In 1992, Austin voters made clear their intent to protect these environmental treasures by passing a "Save Our Springs" water quality ordinance by a 3 to 1 margin.

Developers weren't happy. The Austin water quality ordinance stood in the way of plans by leading developers Gary Bradley and James 'Jim Bob' Moffett, who wanted to build out their thousands of acres of development which lay over the sensitive watershed.

In 1995, during the first legislative session of Governor Bush's first administration, two pieces of legislation, Senate Bill 1017 and House Bill 3193 were filed. Critics charge that these bills were written specifically to benefit certain developers and to overturn local environmental regulations. One bill removed 20,000 acres from the City of Austin's environmental controls. Much of this acreage was owned by Bradley and Moffett. The second bill set up a new governmental entity, carved out of the City of Austin's jurisdiction, which operated with the force of law, but without an elected board which would have had to answer to local citizens.

Despite his campaign rhetoric advocating "local control," Governor Bush ignored the expressed demands of local voters. He allowed both bills to become law despite questions about their constitutionality, opposition from surrounding jurisdictions and widespread community condemnation.

## Supreme Court Overturns Bush Backed Law That Stripped Away Local Control

During Governor Bush's first legislative session, numerous attempts were made to undermine local environmental controls. One of the most blatant attempts was a piece of special interest legislation deceptively named, "Water Quality Protection Zones" (Senate Bill 1017). The goal of the bill, which was directed squarely so as to affect only the City of Austin, was to remove over 8,000 acres from the City's environmental regulation. The area in question had, after 20 years of debate, come under strong water quality protections through the "Save Our Springs" citizen initiative.[185]

Senate Bill 1017 was designed to remove this area from local control. It was sponsored by the real estate affiliate of Freeport-McMoran Inc., an international mining company. The legislation prohibited municipalities from enforcing, "any land use ordinances, rules, or requirements to protect the environment" within a so-called "water protection zone."[186] Big landowners with 1000 acres or more, could designate their land as a "water quality protection zone" without the approval of the state environmental agency. Smaller landowners had to get the agency's approval.

The legislation clearly stated the purpose "is to provide the flexibility necessary to develop the land." Not only did the legislation remove environmental protections, it also removed the real estate from consideration for annexation for 20 years. This was a heavy financial blow to a city that had spent millions on building the infrastructure in the area. An internal memo from the TNRCC, warned legislators against this kind of unconstitutional special interest legislation

"...prohibitions against local laws are intended to combat corruption, personal privileges and meddling in local affairs - or conversely, to prevent a group from dashing to the Capitol to get something their local government would not give them."[187]

Unfortunately, these warnings were ignored. Senate Bill 1017 passed and, with its passage, roughly 20,000 acres of land left the jurisdiction and escaped the environmental regulations of the City of Austin. In July of 2000, the Texas Supreme Court ruled that the law Bush signed was unconstitutional because it gave powers that belonged to the public to private corporations.[188]

## Denying Local Control with More Government

Yet another effort to overturn local control was successful during the 1995 session. House Bill 3193 established the "Southwest Travis County Water District." The water district was created from an area of 8,000 acres on the fragile Barton Springs Edwards aquifer that was previously under the jurisdiction of the City of Austin.

Critics of the legislation believe it was the work of developer Gary Bradley associated with Circle C Properties. The company was developing most of the land within the new water district. Bradley has the distinction of being one of the largest individual defaulters on loans during the 1980's Savings and Loan Crisis, according to Public Employees for Environmental Responsibility. The organization's information also indicates Bradley has been in and out of numerous courtrooms defending charges of fraud and other allegations, and apparently used the Legislature to remove thousands of acres of his land out of the City of Austin's control.[189]

The legislation created a new governmental entity that usurped local control and had unprecedented authority to make rules, annex land, and to issue bonds. This nine-member commission was appointed by the Governor, not elected by local citizens. In fact, it prohibited creation of local governments or political subdivisions even if approved by all the landowners—unless the hand picked commissioners for the "Water District" approved.

In addition, the law removed thousands of acres from strong local environmental controls, it gave the Southwest Travis County Water District power to supercede the authority of surrounding local governments on all issues related to water.

As with Senate Bill 1017, House Bill 3193 passed despite strong local opposition. Governor George Bush ignored public outcry and appeals from a broad-based coalition of local community groups and allowed the Bill to become law. A spokesman for Governor Bush said he was interested in Austin's local water quality issues because, "He's trying to keep bureaucrats in Washington from telling Central Texans what to do with their water and their environment."[190]

House Bill 3193, that Governor Bush allowed to become law, was later found to be unconstitutional by both a state district court and the state court of appeals.[191]

"Local control" is a potent political slogan. However, Governor Bush defines "local control," not as control by the locals, but control by the local contributors to the Bush campaign.

### Bush Donors Associated with Circle C and Freeport-McMoran

| | |
|---|---|
| Armbrust & Brown (lobbyists) | $1,000 |
| Gary Bradley | $3,500 |
| Jim Bob Moffett | $21,000 |
| Stan Schlueter (lobbyist) | $5,000 |
| Strasburger & Price (lobbyists) | $2,500 |
| **TOTAL** | **$33,000** |

Source: Public Employees for Environmental Responsibility

# Bush's Stewardship
## *Conserving or Consuming Public Lands*

Since George W. Bush set his sights on the Presidency, he has made a number of campaign promises that, if elected President, he would support land and wildlife conservation.  However, many conservation organizations are highly skeptical.  Bush's interest in conservation seems newfound and politically motivated to help his presidential bid.  Why, they asked, would he support issues and causes at the national level that he has completely ignored during the time he has served as Governor to Texas.

> *" I want to leave behind a state that is as beautiful for my daughters and for your children as it was for us.  I want our legacy to be one of personal responsibility and good stewardship of our land and resources."*
> --Bush campaign speech, May 2000

Although he took office in 1995, Governor Bush gave little attention to conservation issues until he launched his Presidential campaign in early 1999.  As his record in Texas shows, his interest in conservation issues was not only late in coming, but lacking in substance as well.

## The Legacy of Under-funded and Decaying Parks

Texans, like most Americans, love their parks and want to protect their natural resources.  Texas lawmakers and its Governor have not made protecting these resources a priority.  Following a ten-month review of the Texas Parks and Wildlife Department, the largest newspaper in the state's capitol concluded, "The State isn't keeping up with its stewardship role."  The May 2000 editorial in *the Austin American Statesman* also said, "The outlook for

Texans who love their land looks anything but promising at the moment." The state park system is threatened by, "inadequate repair budgets, thin staffing, gaps in stewardship, pork-barrel politics and a failure to acquire more." [192]

The sad shape of the Texas park system is old news. Texas has remained near the bottom in the rankings of state park expenditures since George W. Bush became governor in 1995. Texas parks make up less than one-half of one percent of the state's total land area and have been overwhelmed by a population expected to double in the next 50 years.

While other states are spending millions to acquire new lands for parks, the state of Texas hasn't pursued a bond issue to expand its park system "since LBJ was president and Elvis and Priscilla got hitched in Las Vegas, in 1967," according to the *Austin American Statesman* editorial.

In 1997, the Texas Parks and Wildlife Department estimated that it would cost *$75 million* to address the park system's most urgent needs, including health, safety, environmental and structural problems. The $75 million figure includes $50 million for water/wastewater, $5 million for Americans with Disabilities Act compliance and $20 million for critical repairs needed at state parks, fish hatcheries, wildlife management areas and other sites.[193] In an emergency action that same year, the legislature approved $60 million in revenue bond authority to begin addressing these critical needs.[194]

Even with the emergency funding measures of 1997, the park system has remained in dire need. A 1998 state audit concluded that an additional $10.1 million in annual funding was needed to adequately maintain park operations. The audit found that the annual budget for state parks covered only 80 percent of what is needed to run them.[195] A 1998 Texas A&M University study ranked Texas 49th in per capita spending on state parks. And, a 1999 Texas Historical Commission study said that Texas historical sites, which make up nearly a third of the park system, needed a $24 million boost for repairs, staffing, and other needs.

To meet the needs identified in these reports, the Texas Parks and Wildlife Department asked the legislature for an additional $35 million in funding in 1999.[196] However, the department received only a fraction of the additional money it sought. As a result, Texas still sits near the bottom in the state rankings of park expenditures.

Governor Bush has contributed to this situation by failing to support proposals which would ensure adequate funding for the Parks and Wildlife Department. As a result, there was a staggering backlog of $186 million dollars in unfunded maintenance chores in 1999 and the disabling of new park acquisitions.[197] This cut in state park funding occurred despite the fact that Parks and Wildlife's annual operating budget increased $1.2 million. The increase resulted mostly through the addition of funds for Landowner Incentive Program to pay for habitat improvement on private property.

With limited funding, the pace of repairs in the state park system has not kept up with the rate of decay – or eliminated the backlog of needed repairs.[198] Not only has the lack of funding prevented the purchase of new lands to expand the park system but, it has prevented the use of lands *donated* to the Parks and Wildlife. As an example, the state was given the Chinati Mountains close to Big Bend National Park in 1996. However, the lands have remained closed, in part because of the lack of operational funds.[199]

## Missing the Meaning of "Stewardship"

Clearly, "the good stewardship of our land and resources," which Governor Bush professes to support, should certainly include adequate public funding for the decaying parks system. However, there is little to indicate Bush's support for this funding.

In Governor Bush's June 1999 "State of the State" address, he spoke to a long list of issues that are important to him, including family values, tort reform, crime, trade, education, and neighborhood quality of life. However, he made no reference to state parks or the conservation of public lands. The closest he came was only to say, "And I propose that we encourage private landowners to conserve land, plant trees, protect wildlife and improve water quality."

The way Governor Bush has encouraged private landowners has been to give them money. Large private property owners who agree to protect habitats for endangered and other threatened species are given public funds through the Texas Landowner Incentive Program.

While educating and assisting private landowners who want to care for our natural resources may be worthwhile, the public doesn't have use of these private lands. Governor Bush fails to mention that our precious natural resources can also be protected by adequately funding and expanding the state park system.

As of August 2000, the web site for the Governor's Office, which lists all of Bush's "news releases" and "initiatives," has nothing to indicate his support for increasing Texas Parks and Wildlife funding. The web site only mentions Governor Bush's efforts to secure funds for the "Landowner Incentive Program." Also mentioned is the Lone Star Legacy Campaign, which Governor Bush initiated in 1998. But this program seeks funding for parks, wildlife management areas, and fish hatcheries from private endowments, not from public funds.

Governor Bush's only mention of increased public funding for Texas Parks and Wildlife is a reference to the $60 million in bonds authorized by the legislature in 1997 and the $10 million appropriated in 1999. However, there is nothing to indicate Governor Bush exercised leadership and advocated for these emergency stop-gap funding measures.

Not only has Governor Bush failed in the past to use the power of his office to ensure adequate funding for the Parks and Wildlife Department, there is nothing to indicate he intends to do so in the future.

He has yet to voice support for the recommendations of a "Sunset Commission" of the legislature, which recognized the importance of the Texas Parks and Wildlife Department. After an exhaustive review, the commission recommended that lawmakers consider several options for permanently increasing the department's budget. One would be to remove the cap on the amount of sporting goods sales tax Parks and Wildlife receives and, have the legislature set the cap each biennium. Gov. Bush was silent on the proposal and it never even got a legislative hearing.[200] Another option, which has yet to receive Bush's support, would allow Texas voters to consider a new series of general obligation bonds to acquire and develop park and conservation lands.

Instead of using the power of his office to ensure adequate funding for parks and wildlife programs, Governor Bush seems to be taking a wait and see attitude. In February of 2000, he appointed a special Conservation Task Force, "to recommend a strategic course for conserving Texas natural resources and promoting outdoor recreation in the 21st century and beyond." To head the Task Force Bush picked Carol Dinkins, a partner in the law firm of Vinson and Elkins. Principals in her firm, which represents some of the largest industrial polluters in Texas, together made the largest contribution to Bush's presidential campaign as of September 1999.[201]

While the recommendations of the legislative Sunset Commission are awaiting Governor Bush's support, the recommendations of his Conservation Task Force aren't due until November 1, 2000—when the presidential election will take place.

## Our National Parks: What Trouble Lies Ahead

Our national parks, like the state parks in Texas, are in trouble and in need of more funding. The same exploding urban population that overwhelms the Texas park system is placing increasing demands on our national parks. The National Park Service estimates immediate repair and maintenance needs in the billions. Other unmet needs including land restoration, employee housing, and purchasing private lands in park boundaries will require more funding.

According to Bush's presidential campaign, he "supports alleviating the substantial repair and improvement backlog facing our national parks, wildlife refuges and other public lands." However, Bush's Presidential Campaign web site, which identifies his "environmental proposals," makes no mention of funding for national parks. Like the web site of his Texas Governor's office, it only mentions funding which goes to private landowners. Bush's proposal for the nation, is to establish a $50 million Landowner Incentive Program that will channel funds to these private landowners, not to public parks or other public lands.

The likelihood that our national parks would be adequately funded under Bush's Presidency is doubtful given his lack of support for the Texas park system which continues to suffer from a huge maintenance backlog of tens of millions of dollars.[202]

Looking at Bush's record in Texas and reading between the lines of his campaign statements, it becomes clear that the prospect of acquiring new public lands under a Bush presidency is also dim. According to Bush, "We have seen millions of acres of land declared off-limits and designated national monuments just like that, with no real public involvement and no regard for the people affected by these decrees."[203]

Based on Bush's poor record of limiting public involvement in decisions of state government, one can only conclude that his real objection is the setting aside of lands for national monuments.[204] Bush has even indicated he might try to remove some of the national designations that were made during President Clinton's administration.[205]

While George W. Bush has been governor of Texas, state purchases of new parkland has come to a virtual halt—even though only 3 percent of the land in Texas is preserved for public use.[206] This should come as no surprise since the Republican Party Platform, which Bush embraced during his 1994 campaign for governor, objected to "the vast acquisition of Texas lands by conservation groups and government agencies."[207]

George W. Bush's "hand's off" attitude towards government raises serious concerns that he will limit government's role in preserving and protecting our nation's natural resources. In an April 2000 campaign speech he said;

*"We have a national consensus about the importance of conservation. But problems arise when leaders reject partnership, and rely solely on*

*the power of Washington on regulations, penalties,
and dictation from afar."*

Bush's hostility to the role of the federal
government is made even clearer when he said, "This
Washington-centered mindset breeds resentment and
needless conflict. It creates a false choice, overlooking
private and local efforts."[208]

Partnerships between government and private
concerns can benefit everyone, but not when they
represent the abdication of governmental responsibilities
to private concerns with interests that conflict with those
of the general public. The so-called "partnerships" formed
under Bush's administrations (in Texas) have been stacked
with business interests and have included little or no
representation from the general public.

Conservation groups have a legitimate concern that
the "partnership" between government and the private
business concerns that George W. Bush strongly advocates,
will translate into private profits at the public's expense.

## Bush Privatization Agenda
## The Commercialization of Texas State Parks

While our public lands represent an irreplaceable
resource and a source of affordable recreation for all
Americans, they are also seen as potential money making
opportunities by private business interests. In the words
of U.S. Supreme Court Justice William O. Douglas, in his
classic, *Farewell to Texas*, "The private concerns see national
and state parks in terms of private enterprise-money-
making-schemes, not nature trails, but amusement
centers."

Dramatic changes in the Texas Park system
proposed under Governor Bush's administration have led

some to fear the state's traditionally rustic state park system may soon be sold to the highest bidder.[209] Under the pretense that state park visitors demand more comfortable overnight accommodations, Texas Parks and Wildlife Department has begun opening-up state parks to private businesses and corporations from the hospitality industry.

Texas parks have had a long commitment to fostering public awareness of the outdoors without excessive dependence on modern conveniences. However, in 1999, Parks and Wildlife quietly solicited proposals from potential investors and resort development firms. Top priority is given to park development schemes with a potential for "revenue generation to both benefit the Texas Parks and Wildlife Department and the program operator."[210]

Allowing private resorts on state lands is not a new idea for Texas Parks and Wildlife. In the 1960's a proposal was approved in a closed-door session which would have transformed Meridian State Park into a members only country club. The project was blocked by a lawsuit brought by the National Audubon Society and NAACP, which filed to protect the wildlife habitat and to prevent de facto segregation. More recently, Parks and Wildlife used $500,000 in federal park improvement funds to expand a golfing facility at Bastrop State Park.[211]

Federal-state funds for Governor Bush's much heralded "Landowner Incentive Program" have not been without controversy. These funds are supposed to be used to protect habitats for endangered or threatened species. However, according to Public Employees for Environmental Responsibility (PEER), they have sometimes been used to subsidize the development of an eco-tourism business on private property.[212] In fact, when the public watchdog organization asked to see *all* of the records associated with the Landowner Incentive Program, they were denied. A formal complaint was filed by Public Employees For Environmental Responsibility, alleging criminal violations of the Federal Clean Water Act, National Environmental Protection Act, the Endangered Species Act, and the Migratory Birds Treaty.[213]

## Open Season in Public Parks

Other controversial programs in Texas include closing state parks to allow deer hunting and privatizing White-tailed Deer breeding. This allows landowners to produce large-antlered bucks for private, for-profit trophy-hunts.[214]

During the 1999-2000 hunting season, revenue-starved state parks closed down a total of 318 days to accommodate the minority of Texans who are licensed to hunt. Parks and Wildlife's explanation for these closures stated simply that these hunts occur on weekdays when the general public rarely uses the parks.

While there may be an argument for controlling the size of deer herds within some parks, decisions to allow hunting should be based on the need to do so—not the need for revenue or a select group's desire for sole access. Pedernales Falls State Park, one of the sites considered for resort development, closed 37 days during the holidays during December and January of 1999-2000 calendar years[215]

## Public Lands - Private Profits

Under a George W. Bush presidency, our national forests may lose many protections they have long been guaranteed. In a June 2000 campaign statement, candidate Bush promised "to cut more trees, abandon talk of breaching dams and work closely with traditional local power structures."[216]

He also promised to try and reverse the Clinton administration's plan to protect more than 43 million acres of road-less national forest land. George W. Bush said it would be good for the economy "to look at a reasonable amount of board-feet to be harvested out of northwestern timberlands." He also criticized the Clinton administration's 1993 Forest Summit in Portland, which resulted in "a major reduction in the amount of board feet that we harvest."

George W. Bush says, *"The demands of development have sometimes been harsh on the natural world and its inhabitants...But it need not be so if we bring to conservation the same vision and ingenuity we bring to development."*

Catchy statements like this are no doubt meant to appeal to conservationists and developers alike. It is telling that Bush wishes to bring the vision and ingenuity of development to conservation. He says this in the same breath in which he admits that the "demands of development" have been "harsh on the natural world and its inhabitants." If he indeed cared to learn from those mistakes, he should acknowledge the need to bring the principals of conservation and protection *to* development. George W. Bush's record indicates that he lacks a varied perspective and he lacks balance. It now appears that he lacks empathy for the victims of development's "harsh" actions, as well.

# Using Public Waters
## *As Industry's Private Sewers*

In 1972 the Federal Water Pollution Control Act was passed to control the discharge of pollutants to surface waters from most municipal and industrial sources. The law established a permitting program, which was administered by the Environmental Protection Agency. In many states, EPA delegated the authority to run this program, called the National Pollutant Discharge Elimination System (NPDES program), to state environmental agencies. In mid 1998, Texas was only one of seven states who were still not allowed to run the program within it own borders.

The Texas environmental agency tried at least eight times, beginning first in 1979, to gain authorization from the EPA to administer the NPDES program. Eight times Texas' application was rejected by the EPA based on findings that the state's water pollution program was inadequate. In every rejection, the EPA expressed concern about the lack of the State's adequate enforcement.

In 1996, after George W. Bush had been governor more than a year, the Bush appointed TNRCC commissioners tried again to get authority over the NPDES program. The EPA wrote three letters to the state, one stating 70 pages of deficiencies. Again, the EPA rejected the state proposal. As in the past, EPA's concerns included the state's inadequate enforcement program. Several aspects of the program have been criticized, including the lack of resources, lack of commitment and the lack of assurances that the public could participate in enforcement decisions. In 1998, the EPA also criticized Texas law, which, unlike federal law, allowed a wide range of civil and criminal defenses for pollution violators.

The TNRCC finally drafted legislation that revised almost every provision of Texas law relating to enforcement of water pollution and other related programs. The proposal by the agency did not eliminate, or even change, those sections of the law that provided the extra defenses to polluters or the provisions that limited public participation in enforcement decisions.

Instead of earnestly trying to address EPA's concerns and strengthen the Texas water pollution program, the TNRCC pressured the EPA to weaken the program it was willing to accept. The letter from the state environmental agency to EPA suggested there was no more room for negotiation.[217]

A broad coalition of organizations and individuals urged EPA *not* to approve a weaker program. In May of 1998, Texas Land Commissioner Gary Mauro personally wrote to EPA administrator Carol Browner, stating;

> "I have observed with interest, the past failures of the Texas water pollution agencies to develop a program that could qualify for EPA approval...The deficiencies in the states' pollution enforcement laws and enforcement efforts and the barriers to public participation in water pollution decisions have been a valid basis for EPA's rejection of the Texas program..."

The Texas Land Commissioner 's letter to EPA also summarized the declining effectiveness of the state environmental agency. This decline continued after George W. Bush became governor in 1995.

"Moreover, there are indications that during the last few years, the Texas water pollution program has gotten worse. Funding for the TNRCC water pollution program has dropped. As a result, TNRCC admitted this year it is only inspecting 30 percent of the wastewater facilities in Texas each year. In 1996 penalties for water pollution violations were at a 10-year low. Efforts by

TNRCC to streamline the permitting process have created even greater barriers to public participation. TNRCC has yet to develop an adequate water quality standards program for all Texas rivers, lakes and bays."

In September of 1998, EPA backed down from its earlier demands for a strong Texas water pollution enforcement program. Governor Bush and his TNRCC were finally given the authority to operate the federal program within the State.

## Blaming God for the Pollution

An example of the inability or failure of the state environmental agency to enforce water pollution laws can be found by examining the permitting of Exxon's disposal of waste into Galveston Bay. Exxon failed to invest in an adequate wastewater treatment system for its massive Baytown refinery and chemical plant complex. As a result, untreated wastewater sometimes backed up in the treatment system and was dumped into Galveston Bay. The frequent discharges of millions of gallons of wastewater contained oil, benzene, and other chemicals. Some of the daytime discharges were discovered and classified as "oil spills" by the Coast Guard. In September of 1995, after Texans United and Baytown citizens challenged Exxon's state discharge permit, Governor Bush's appointees sided with Exxon and excused the pollution of public waters as an "Act of God" associated with rainfall.

After the Bush-appointed TNRCC commissioners allowed Exxon's untreated wastewater dumping to continue, citizens turned to the EPA and the courts for help. Attorney Robert Fugate, a former employee of the U.S. Environmental Protection Agency's Water Enforcement Section, said the state's refusal to take action against Exxon was an example of the politically appointed

TNRCC commissioners' reluctance to get tough with powerful corporate polluters.

Robert Fugate, along with Houston attorney Valorie Davenport and Washington, D.C.-based Trial Lawyers for Public Justice, represented citizens in their legal efforts to stop Exxon's pollution. In March of 1996, a federal lawsuit was filed against Exxon utilizing provisions of the federal Clean Water Act allowing citizens to enforce the law when the government fails to do so. There were no citizen enforcement options under state environmental laws.

After the citizens went to court, the EPA finally took the first step towards banning Exxon's untreated discharges in December of 1996. The EPA found that Exxon's discharges were due to an inadequate wastewater treatment system. Exxon was forced to improve the system at an approximate cost of $1 million. Although the rain may have been God's doing, Exxon was responsible for failing to prevent toxic discharges into the Gulf of Mexico.

In April of 1998, after years of citizen protest and an expensive uphill battle against Exxon *and* TNRCC, the federal court ordered Exxon to pay over $100,000 in legal fees to the citizen's attorneys.

In the end, our public waters were protected because of federal intervention, something that George W. Bush considers to be "heavy-handed." Our public waters were also protected because of litigation, which George W. Bush considers to be "unnecessary." It is not surprising that Exxon's Political Action Committee contributed over $24,000 toward Bush's campaigns for governor from 1993 through 1998.[218]

# George W. Bush
## *Silencing the First Amendment*

On August 30, 2000, a state District Court ruled against Governor Bush after he asked to be dropped from a lawsuit brought by citizens who were arrested for peacefully protesting outside the Governor's mansion.[219] The judge's ruling was based on his belief that the Texas Governor has a general responsibility to ensure that the State police enforce the law and act in a lawful manner. Governor Bush, who appoints the commissioners of the state police, claimed to have no such responsibility. The lawsuit was filed in 1999 after citizens were arrested, strip searched, and jailed. The head of the Governor's "Protective Detail," after meeting with Governor Bush, enacted the "new policy" leading to the arrests. Governor Bush then publicly supported the policy and the jailing of citizens.

For years, the public sidewalk outside the fence surrounding the Governor's mansion has been a traditional site of public protest. This has been true under Democratic and Republican governors alike. Even the state police officers testified they were aware of no previous arrests of peaceful protestors. Historically, citizens have gathered outside the mansion to freely express their views—at least until Governor Bush began to campaign for the Presidency.

In early 1999, when Governor Bush began entertaining an entourage of political leaders and media representatives, unwritten "new rules" were adopted governing the public's use of the sidewalk. Governor Bush and the head of his Protective Detail met and discussed the "new" rules. After this discussion, citizens were arrested. Governor Bush then publicly approved of the new rules and the arrests.

Lieutenant Escalante, who heads Bush's Protective Detail, says he can remember nothing about his discussion with the Governor. Governor Bush refused to testify under oath about his discussion with Escalante and others concerning the rules and the arrests.

Governor Bush says he had nothing to do with the policy or the arrests. However, few people believe that highly publicized arrests in front of the Governor's Mansion, initiated by the Governor's own Protective Detail, would have taken place without the Governor's approval. One officer testified that the Governor was informed whenever a demonstration took place.

The Governor and his "Protective Detail" failed to follow the required process for approval of "new rules" governing the use of the public sidewalk. They also selectively enforced the rules, allowing some protesters to stay on the sidewalk while others were forced to leave under threat of arrest. The judge, who denied the Governor's motion to be dismissed from the lawsuit, was shown photographs of protesters waving the Confederate flag and protesting that it be flown over the Capitol. The 'Confederate' protesters were *allowed* to do the same thing, in the same place, that landed environmentalists in jail.

All of the environmental protesters were focussing attention on Bush's environmental policies and campaign contributions from big business polluters. Dierdra Tinker, a PTA mother, was handcuffed and placed in the back seat of a patrol car. Mrs. Tinker was arrested, apparently because she did not move fast enough (off the sidewalk) to satisfy the demands of the state trooper threatening her with arrest. She was released only after her companions pleaded that she needed to pick her children up from daycare. Along with other citizens from the organization "Downwinders at Risk," she had driven several hours from the Dallas area to protest a hazardous waste-burning cement kiln near her home. The continued burning was allowed by Bush's environmental agency appointees.

A little over two weeks later, on March 29, 1999 about 50 people from across the state met at the Governor's mansion sidewalk to peacefully protest Bush's role in a "voluntary" pollution reduction program for some of the largest industrial polluters in the state. All protesters were ordered off the sidewalk, including women, children, and mothers pushing baby carriages. They were directed further away from the mansion to a public sidewalk across the street. Every protestor except one did as ordered for fear of being of being arrested. They didn't want to miss the chance to testify at a legislative hearing.

Texans United Education Fund Director, Rick Abraham (the author), was left alone on the sidewalk with the Governor's Protective Detail and state troopers. For the atrocity of carrying a sign that read, *"Air Pollution Kills,"* Abraham was arrested, handcuffed, strip searched and jailed for twelve hours. He was charged with "blocking an entrance." In fact, the entrance to the Mansion was closed and no one was present to be blocked.

## A Citizen Speaks and the Governor Refuses to Listen

The following letter was sent to Governor Bush, received by his office, and marked with a notation that a response was not necessary.

April 10, 1999

Dear Governor Bush,

On Monday March 29, approximately 50 citizens from around the state held a news conference and protest rally outside our Governor's mansion. We held the event at the mansion, your home, because *you* are advocating legislation that would allow more pollution in the homes of average Texas families. You want to continue the legal loophole for "grandfathered" industrial polluters that exempts them from full permits and modern pollution controls. Representatives from environmental, labor, and citizen organizations attended the protest rally to publicly express opposition to your legislation.

When citizens first gathered on the public sidewalk adjacent to the mansion, a representative from the Governor's Protection Detail of the Capitol Police came and demanded to see identification. He threatened citizens with arrest if they did not move to the sidewalk across the street. The entrance to the mansion was closed and the sidewalk was *not* being blocked. Even so, I was arrested, charged with "blocking an entrance," and jailed overnight.

Since there was a hearing on pollution legislation that same afternoon, most citizens did not want to take the chance of being arrested. They attended the hearing in large numbers and it lasted into the early hours of the next morning. Citizens should not have had to choose, as I did, between exercising their right to protest and testifying at the hearing.

Others have been arrested for protesting outside the Governor's mansion, including a PTA mother who dared to speak out against pollution several weeks earlier. You must speak out against these illegal arrests. It is wrong to allow powerful corporate polluters to avoid pollution laws at the same times citizens' rights to protest pollution are being violated. Our first amendment rights, like our pollution laws, should not be selectively enforced on the basis of who gives you money and support.

This letter is to ask you to inform those associated with your "protection" detail that the constitutional rights of citizens do not end at the public sidewalk in front of our Governor's mansion. Protecting you from public *criticism* is not a proper function of the Capitol Police who are paid with public funds.

We respect your right to advocate the programs you choose and we certainly expect you to respect the rights of Texans to oppose those programs. Lawful public protest is a part of the process by which public policy is debated and decided. We hope you will remember this as our Governor - and never forget it should you become President.

Citizens will no doubt hold other lawful demonstrations outside the Governor's mansion. We can only hope that you will recognize and support our first amendment rights with the same level of enthusiasm that you support "grandfathered" corporate polluters. We would appreciate a copy of your letter to the Capitol Police regarding this matter.

Sincerely,

Rick Abraham
Executive Director
Texans United Education Fund

The letter was received by the Governor's office and a decision was made not to answer it.[220] After the letter was received by the Governor's office, the arrests continued.

On April 19, 1999, a third environmental protest was held outside the Governor's mansion on the public sidewalk. This time four people were arrested while standing on the edge of the sidewalk far from the entrance to the Governor's mansion. They stood with their backs against a brick wall to make sure there was room for pedestrians to pass, even though no pedestrians were present.

Among those arrested were Michael Covington and Karen Sloan, two refinery workers from Crown Central Petroleum, a notorious polluter, and a heavy contributor to Governor Bush's election campaigns. Also arrested were Roger Baker, a member of the Green Party and, for a second time, Texans United's Rick Abraham. This arrest came after the Governor had received and decided not to respond to Abraham's letter. All of those arrested, including Karen Sloan, were again charged with "blocking an entrance." They were jailed, strip-searched, and made to sleep on the floor in overcrowded jail cells.

Later, on the same day after the third set of arrests were made, Teighlor Darr, a reporter for Austin radio station KJFK-FM, went back to the Governor's Mansion sidewalk. She also carried a sign. Her sign simply read "I like Bush." When approached by the Governor's Protective Detail, she explained that her action was a "support" and not a "protest." She then was freely allowed, for two hours, to walk up and down the exact same sidewalk. This occurred on the same sidewalk where the environmental protesters had been arrested only hours before.[221] She was neither jailed, nor strip-searched. Her use of the public sidewalk to voice "support" for the Governor went unchallenged—even as the protesters of Bush's environmental policies sat behind bars.

On May 25, 1999, environmental protesters returned to the Governor's Mansion sidewalk, this time joined by Francis "Sissy" Farenthold, a former state legislator and a candidate for Texas Governor in the 1970's. This time only Jim Baldauf, a Texans United Board member, was arrested. Mr. Baldauf, as was the case with others who had been arrested before, was walking on the sidewalk alone. No one was near him who would be inconvenienced in any way. However, rather than arrest Ms. Farenthold, who continued to walk on the sidewalk in the presence of news media, the police decided to forgo any more arrests.

Jim Baldauf, who was arrested for doing exactly what Ms. Farenthold and others were allowed to do, was handcuffed, strip-searched and jailed for 24 hours – without ever being charged. The other protesters arrested in March and April of 1999 were never prosecuted. The Travis County Attorney determined there was insufficient evidence. Videotapes of the arrests clearly show that citizens were doing nothing more than peacefully exercising their constitutionally protected rights.

## Governor Bush: Keeper or Slayer
## of the First Amendment

In August of 1999 Texans United and others filed a lawsuit against the Department of Public Safety (state police) and Governor George W. Bush.[222] The lawsuit challenges the constitutionality of the new, unwritten policy and seeks to restore free speech rights to the public sidewalk outside the Governor's Mansion. To date, both Governor Bush and the Department of Public Safety (state police) have chosen to maintain and defend their unwritten policy against protests.

Following the arrests on April 19, Governor Bush held a news conference with visiting New York Mayor Rudolph Giulliani. He said he approved of the policy governing the use of the sidewalk and the arrests of the protesters. The Governor said, "People have just gotta understand what the rules are."[223] However, as of September 2000, the "rules" are still not in writing and seem subject to different interpretations. According to citizens' Attorney David Kahne, "the courts have previously held that such unwritten rules are unconstitutional because they give 'unbridled discretion' to authorities who can use them to silence their critics."

## Avoiding Responsibility and
## Dodging Sworn Testimony

Governor Bush's deposition was requested to determine the extent of his role in establishing the unconstitutional policy. If he played no such role, his sworn deposition could have gone far to establish his innocence. Instead, Governor Bush refused to be deposed and avoided having to answer questions under oath. He did so even though he criticized President Clinton for attempting to do the exact same thing.

"Governor Bush thinks he's above the law," said Jim Baldauf, one of the arrested citizens. "Governor Bush brags about 'leadership' and preaches about 'personal responsibility' and then says, 'I'm not responsible.' According to Baldauf, who was jailed for 24 hours without being charged, "He refused to testify under oath in the 'Funeral-gate' case, he refused to give a sworn deposition in our case and he's refused to answer specific questions about his military record and his drug and alcohol use."

The citizens who dared to file the lawsuit against Governor Bush and the state police were grilled by the Governor's lawyers about previous arrests that may have occurred over their lifetime – including any related to drug and alcohol use. Governor George W. Bush, who so freely approved of the citizens being jailed, could rightfully be asked if he knows what it's like to be deprived of his freedom. Has *he* ever been arrested? How many times, and what for? Some people speculate that the fear of being asked such questions is one reason he refused to testify.

Not only has Governor Bush and the Department of Public Safety, headed by Bush's appointees, sought to deny the right to free speech and peaceable assembly, they have also tried to undermine citizens' rights to freedom of association. The state's lawyers have tried to obtain the lists of all members of Texans United—and the names of its contributors. Some members and contributors actually work for industrial polluters and/or government agencies. If the names of the members employed by polluters were disclosed, these people would almost surely face recriminations. Forcing the names of members and contributors of private organizations to be made a matter of public record could have a chilling effect on citizen participation. The courts historically have recognized this risk and have routinely protected this information from forced disclosure.

Rather than using the power of his office to ensure citizens' free speech rights are protected, Governor Bush has used law enforcement officers, paid by taxpayer dollars, to curtail free speech and jail his more vocal critics. He apparently forgot that public debate on his and every politicians records, is at the heart of this country's freedom.

Even *if* Bush didn't cook up the new rules for protesters, he did not *object* to them. Neither has he objected to his lawyers prying into the memberships of private organizations. This says he doesn't understand constitutional rights, or he doesn't believe in them. Either prospect is frightening.

# Notes and References

1. "Lone Star Election Laws," report released by the U.S. Public Interest Research Group Education Fund and Texans for Public Justice (www.onr.com/tpj), July 2000.

2. "Lone Star Election Laws," report released by the U.S. Public Interest Research Group Education Fund and Texans for Public Justice (www.onr.com/tpj), July 2000.

3. Texas Election Code Section 253.034 prohibits statewide officeholders and member of the Legislature from accepting contributions while the Legislature is in session. This law is designed to prevent conflicts of interests between parties with issues before the Legislature and elected officials who are in the process of making state law. Under the state election code, an elected official who receives a contribution during the legislative session is required to return the donation to the contributor no later than 30 days after the date the funds are received.

4. Reported in the *Austin American Statesman*, "Polluters' donations to Bush criticized," May 1, 1999. (www.austin 360.com/statesman)

5. Alan Miller, *Los Angeles Times*, "Texas Corporate Interests Financed Bulk of Bush Races," July 14, 1999. (www.latimes.com/)

6. Public Research Works (www..foree.com/prw).

7. The report analyzes the Pioneers made public by Bush as of July 15, 2000. It classifies them by their business and ideological interests, tracks the total money each spends on politics, and provides individual profiles of each of the 212. Among the findings of The Bush Pioneer report: 133 Pioneers are business executives, George Bush appointed 16 Pioneers to state government posts, 14 have spent the night at the Governor's mansion in Austin, 13 represent polluter interests, 35 have benefited from corporate-welfare, 26 have been involved in one or more campaign finance-related scandals, and 20 Pioneers have kept the revolving door between government and industry spinning.

The 212 identified Pioneers have raised a minimum of $21.2 million in hard money for Bush's presidential effort. These 212 individuals also contributed $2.3 million to Bush's gubernatorial campaigns, $7.1 million in hard money to federal candidates and PACs and $4.1 million in soft money contributions to federal political party committees since the '96 election cycle.

The top 5 individual money movers among the Pioneers (total federal money since the '96 election cycle plus money to Bush's gubernatorial campaigns) are: A.G. Spanos , $877,450; Sam Fox, $831,733; Kenneth Lay, $574,550; Tom Loeffler, $495,424; and, Louis A. Beecherl, Jr., $446,350. Among the 212 Pioneers, the top overall contributors to Bush's gubernatorial campaigns are: Charles J. Wyly, Jr., $210,273; Dennis R. Berman, $175,000; Louis A. Beecherl, Jr., $154,000; Tom Loeffler, $141,000; and, Richard Heath, $124,449. Eighty-four companies controlled by or employing these 212 individuals contributed an additional $21 million in soft money contributions to political party committees since the '96 election cycle, $15.5 million to the Republicans, $5.5 million to the Democrats. Sixty-six of the Pioneers hail from Texas. The other Bush state, Florida, claims the next largest batch with 21. California has produced 14 and Michigan 12. No other state is in the double-digits. The Bush Pioneer report is available at Texans for Public Justice. (www.tpj.org/pioneers/)

8. August 2000 interview with Bill Medaille, an analyst for Texans For Public Justice who attempted to review Governor George W. Bush's campaign filings.

9. "Playing politics with campaign contributions," Editorial by Alan Bernstein, *Houston Chronicle*, July 26, 1998. (www.chron.com/)

10. Texans for Public Justice Report on Bush "Pioneer" fundraisers can be viewed at (www.tpj.org/pioneers/).

11. Harris County has consistently ranked at the top , or near,the top of the national list for toxic air releases according to EPA's annual Toxic Release Inventory. In 1999, Harris County recorded eight of the ten highest ozone levels in the country.

12. According to environmental group representatives, including Texans United Education Fund, who participated in meetings with elected officials and industry representatives to discuss legislation consolidating Texas environmental agencies.

13. *Time Magazine*, February 21, 2000.

14. The reporting requirements for the U S Environmental Protection Agency Toxic Release Inventory (TRI) changed several times since they reporting began in 1987. For example, certain chemicals have been taken off the list of chemicals to be reported and other chemicals have been added.

15. Reported by the *New York Times*, "On the record: Governor Bush and the Environment," November 9, 1999. (www.latimes.com/).

16. U.S Environmental Protection Agency Toxic Release Inventory; *Houston Chronicle*; "Toxic release ratings drop Texas to fifth / First time since 1993 that state won't top list," May 12, 2000. *Houston Chronicle* Archives (www.chron.com/). See U.S. EPA TRI data at (www.epa.gov/tri98/index.htm).

17. Reported by Alan Miller, *Los Angeles Times*, "Texas Corporate Interests Financed Bulk of Bush Races," July 14, 1999. (www.latimes.com/).

18. EPA data as referenced in Sierra Club's August 8, 2000 News Release taking issue with Governor Bush's claims about the environment. (www.sierraclub.org/chapters/tx/)

19. Reported by Jim Yardley, the *New York Times*, "On the Record: Governor Bush and the Environment," November 9, 1999. (www.nytco.com/)

20. According to Texas Natural Resource Conservation Commission data center, as of August 2000, major metropolitan areas in Texas including Houston/Galveston/Brazoria, Beaumont/Port Arthur, Dallas/Fort Worth and El Paso, are in non-attainment of the one-hour ozone standard.

21. Environmental Protection Agency Toxic Release Inventory released May 11, 2000, (www.epa.gov/tri98/index.htm).

22. Bush's late support for this legislation was reported in numerous news articles including: *Houston Chronicle*, "Facts hard to find political smog: Bush, Gore, media, environmentalists hazy on specifics of city's ozone woes," April 10, 2000; Environment, "Houston refineries are years behind Los Angeles in pollution control. Gore previews likely attack on issue," February 25, 2000; Publicly, Bush had adamantly backed the "voluntary" concept for all grandfathered industrial facilities for more than two years. His media events, held with industry leaders including those from utility companies, praised the "voluntary" program. However, late in the legislative session, with mounting opposition to the voluntary concept, Rep. Steve Wolens from Dallas inserted a provision into a utility deregulation bill that required emission cuts from power plants. It was then that Bush voiced his support for required reductions from power plants. Despite Bush's late support for the idea, television adds by a group called Republicans for Clean Air, which attacked Senator John McCain's air pollution record during the republican primary, claimed that Bush had 'led' the Texas effort to "clamp down on old coal-burning electric power plants."

23. Reported in the *Washington Post*, "George W. Bush: The Texas Record; Evidence Contradicts Claims of Cleaner Air," October 15, 1999. (www.washingtonpost.com).

24. See the American Lung Association Web site: Legislative Agenda: Clean Air (http://www.texaslung.org/). The ALA states, "Senate Bill 766, the Governor's voluntary compliance bill was amended in the House to have all the clean air components the American Lung Association wanted. However, all the amendments were taken off in conference committee. The end result is not enough to close the grandfathered loophole. The bill creates a disincentive to a few large grandfathered polluters to continue their grandfathered status by using the state's clean air fee assessments on tons of pollution emitted. A quick analysis of state emissions inventory data indicates that only eight or nine grandfathered sources of air pollution would be potentially encouraged to come into the permitting process as a result of fees being assessed against them for remaining in a grandfathered status. Thus, the vast majority of the 800 plus grandfathered facilities would not be subject to persuasion to enter the permitting process to avoid assessment of high levels of fees."

25. Alcoa, with single largest source of grandfathered emissions in the Texas, discharged over 100,000 tons annually of pollution according to the Texas Natural Resource Conservation Commissions 1997 Source Survey Report. According to Neil Carman, PhD. of the Lone Star Chapter of the Sierra Club, the carefully worded language in Senate Bill 766 excluded Alcoa by virtue of definitions regarding coal fired facilities. The fact that Alcoa escaped coverage of requirements that applied to other power plants was widely reported in the news media. According to Public Research Works and the Center for Responsive Politics, the principals in the law of Vinson & Elkins, who represented Alcoa, contributed $184,850 to the Bush presidential campaign as of September 1, 1999.

26. "To Little-To Late," a study released in November of 1998 by the Environmental Defense Fund. The report can be viewed at EDF's Web site: (www.edf.org).

27. U.S. EPA Toxic Release Inventory (www.epa.gov/tri98/).

28. Reported in the Statesman, "Polluters' donations to Bush criticized," May 1, 1999. Archives (www.austin 360.com/statesman)

29. EPA data as referenced in Sierra Club August 8, 2000 News Release taking issue with Governor Bush's claims about the environment. (www.sierraclub.org/chapters/tx/).

30. Lone Star Chapter of the Sierra Club news release, "Sierra Club Criticizes Governor Bush's Attempts to 'Greenwash' His Record on Land Conservation," April 11, 2000.(www.sierraclub.org/chapters/tx/).

31. See the Environmental Defense Fund's state-by-state ranking and analysis of oil refinery performance, September 30, 1999. Oil refineries use and release toxic chemicals, sulfur compounds that create odors and cause acid rain, and volatile organic chemicals, which contribute to smog formation. To create the rankings, EDF used publicly reported data for these pollutants to determine the pollution per barrel of oil refined. EDF then identified which of the country's 144 refineries with complete pollution data performed the best and worst for these multiple measures of refinery efficiency. Refineries in Texas, Oklahoma, Montana, Wyoming were ranked the dirtiest. A state-by-state ranking of refinery performance can be found at EDF's Web site:(www.edf.org).

32. Neil Carman Phd., Clean Air Director of the Lone Star Chapter Sierra Club. The TNRCC has been charged with violating Title VI of the Civil Rights Act of 1964, which prohibits discrimination in programs using federal funds. Complaints have charged the agency the agency with a pattern of skewed permitting practices and lax enforcement in pursuing violations at industrial plants across the state. Texas now leads the nation in civil rights (Title VI) complaints filed against a state environmental agency. At least 12 complaints have been filed against the TNRCC with the EPA's Office of Civil Rights since 1994. TNRCC has also been charged with violating an Executive Order on environmental justice, which requires that federal programs and federally funded projects not be allowed to increase "the disproportionate burdens of environmental hazards in communities of color and low-income neighborhoods."

33. Thomas Crowley, Phd. "Science" Journal, July 14, 2000; "Global Warming Solutions," a report by World Wildlife Fund, February 2000. According to a statement released by the Sustainable Energy and Economic Development Coalition and Texas Public Citizen in August 2000, the vast majority of the world's climate scientists agree that the world is warming due to the emission of greenhouse gases from cars, power plants, refineries and other human-controlled sources. Texas is the largest source of global warming emissions in the U.S. If Texas were an independent country, it would rank 7th in the world for carbon emissions. The vast majority of the world's climate scientists agree that the world is warming due to the emission of greenhouse gases from cars, power plants, refineries and other human-controlled sources. Climate experts, including those at Texas A&M University and the University of Texas, consider Texas to be particularly vulnerable to global warming' impacts. The potential effects on Texas include: temperature increases ranging from 3 to 7 degrees (F); an increase in dangerous heat waves; an increase in the frequency and severity of cycles of droughts and floods; a 35% reduction

in fresh water flows in regular years and as much as 85% in drought years; and, the loss of coastal areas flooded by rising seas.

34. *Texas Parks and Wildlife News*, "1997 In Review-TPW's Top 10 News Stories," Dec. 22, 1997.

35. "TNRCC Enforcement: Records or Rhetoric," a report by the Texas Center for Policy Studies (www..texascenter.org/), December 1996; Roth Bennet, *Houston Chronicle*, "Gore's attacks on Bush extend to bashing Texas /Low ranking in social services used as fodder for criticism," May 21, 2000. The article reported Texas was 43rd in natural resources per capita spending ($32.52) in 1998 and 49th in parks/recreation per capita spending ($3 .36) in 1998. (www.chron.com/)

36. Statements from Texas Public Employees for Environmental Responsibility, an alliance of state and federal employees working in pollution control, land management and wildlife protection agencies. (www.txpeer.org).

37. "West Texas Notes," Associated Press Wire Service, February 5, 1998. Bush said. "As I told the Ambassador [from Mexico], much of the discussion is about disposal of, for example, X-rays. And there's tons of X-rays piled up in El Paso hospitals as we speak today," he said. "This is low-level radioactive waste. This is not high-powered plutonium." (www.compassionate.org/sbldf).

38. The letter, which Bush signed on September 23, 1997, was used to build Congressional support for the Texas dumpsite plan that was clearly in trouble; "U.S. House Passes Compact Bill," Sierra Blanca Legal Defense Fund News Release of Oct 7, 1997 (www.compassionate.org/sbldf).

39. Texas Supreme Court Case 98-0685, June 15, 2000; Interview with Attorney Bill Bunch, Executive Director of the Save Our Springs Alliance, September 13, 2000.

40. Senate Bill 1017 was introduced and passed with Governor Bush's signature in the 1995 Texas legislative session.

41. House Bill 3193 was passed without Bush's signature. He did not veto or publicly oppose the legislation. He appointed the commissioners to the newly established governmental entity. According to the Save Our Springs Alliance, these commissioners were the individuals the developers wanted to see in control; Interview with Attorney Bill Bunch, Executive Director of the Save Our Springs Alliance, September 13, 2000.

42 Interview with Attorney Bill Bunch, Executive Director of the Save Our Springs Alliance, September 13, 2000.

43. George W. Bush Presidential Campaign (www.georgewbush.com).

44. George W. Bush Presidential Campaign (www.georgewbush.com).

45. Susan B. Glasser and John Mintz, *Washington Post*, "Bush Capitol Plan to Woo Big Business; First He Wins Over Trade Group Chiefs," August 1, 1999. (www.washingtonpost.com)

46. Alan Miller, *Los Angeles Times*, "Texas Corporate Interests Financed Bulk of Bush Races," July 14, 1999. (www.latimes.com/)

47. Public Research Works (www..foree.com/prw)

48. Statement of Jane Saginaw, EPA Region VI Administrator referenced in Texas Natural Resource Conservation Commission official publication "Natural Outlook," Spring 1997.

49. Texans United et al. v. Exxon Company USA, Civil Action No. H-96-847.

50. Texas Natural Resources Conservation Commission Air Emissions Inventory from Point Source Database made public in October, 1998; "Grandfathered Air Pollution, The Dirty Secret of Texas Industries," a report by the Galveston Houston Association for Smog Prevention and the Lone Star Chapter of the Club, April 1998.

51. "How the Grandfather Loophole Threatens Texas School Children," Second Edition, Sustainable Energy and Economic Development Coalition, 1999. Pollution levels of 18 million cars is calculated from TNRCC data on emissions from grandfathered facilities and EPA data on emissions from an average passenger car.

52. American Lung Association's report, "State of the Air 2000" (http://www.texaslung.org/).

53. "Revisions to the State Implementation Plan for the Control of Ozone Air Pollution," Texas Natural Resource Conservation Commission, February 1998 and August 2000.

54. "Revisions to the State Implementation Plan for the Control of Ozone Air Pollution, Texas Natural Resource Conservation Commission," February 1998 and August 2000.

55. "Revisions to the State Implementation Plan for the Control of Ozone Air Pollution, Texas Natural Resource Conservation Commission," February 1998 and August 2000.

56. Reported in *Houston Chronicle*, "unhealthy' smog recorded," July 7, 2000. (www.chron.com/).

57. American Lung Association's report, "State of the Air 2000." (www.texaslung.org).

58. Study is referenced in American Lung Association's report, "State of the Air 2000" (www.texaslung.org).

59. American Academy of Allergy, Asthma and Immunology news release, "High Ozone Levels Harmful to Respiratory System, Especially for Asthmatics," June 1, 1999.

60. Jim Yardley, The *New York Times*, "On the Record: Governor Bush and the Environment," November 9, 1999. Archives (www.latimes.com/).

61. Bill Dawson, *Houston Chronicle*, "unhealthy' smog recorded," July 7, 2000. Archives (www.chron.com/).

62. National Ambient Air Quality Standards can be reviewed at TNRCC's Web site (tnrcc.state.tx.us/).

63. *Houston Chronicle*, "Something in the Air," August 21, 2000. Archives (www.chron.com/).

64. September 13, 2000 interview with Jane Elioseff, one of the founders of Galveston Houston Association for Smog Prevention who was instrumental in bringing about the publicizing of ozone levels and the issuance of ozone alerts.; The GHASP Web Site is (www.neosoft.com/~ghasp/); Also see Public Employees for Environmental Responsibility, "Bush's quiet little war on the Texas environment: Assault on the regulatory front." (www.texpeer.org).

65. Public Employees for Environmental Responsibility, "Bush's quiet little war on the Texas environment: Assault on the regulatory front." (www.texpeer.org); Also reported in *Washington Post*, "George W. Bush: The Texas Record; Evidence Contradicts Claims of Cleaner Air," October 15, 1999. Archives (www.washingtonpost.com).

66. Letter from Beverly Hartstock, Deputy Director of TNRCC Office of Policy and Regulatory Development to Tom Helms, U.S. Environmental Protection Agency, August 1995.

67. "Bush's quiet little war on the Texas environment: Assault on the regulatory front, The Bush Pollution Plan," Texas Public Employees for Environmental Responsibility: (www.texpeer.org). According to PEER, the Texas Plan also included other changes. It used a rolling eight-hour average to diminish the effects of temperature and meteorology. It limited the data under consideration to include no more than five exceedances (unsafe levels) per year averaged over a three-year period; and deleted the high and low years (from the most recent five years) to determine the three year average.

68. Texas Natural Resource Conservation Commission official publication "Natural Outlook," Spring 1997. The document can be viewed on the web site of Texas Public Employees for Environmental Responsibility: (www.texpeer.org)

70. Texas Natural Resource Conservation Commission official publication "Natural Outlook," Spring 1997.

71. In a 1993 article in the New England Journal of Medicine, researchers reported on a study following more than 8000 persons in six different locations over a period of seventeen years. In areas with varying levels of PM2.5-- particles with a diameter of 2.5 microns or less, small enough to penetrate deeply into the lungs. After controlling for other factors, they found that the risk of early death in high level areas to be increased by 26 percent over that in areas with the lowest levels. (Dockery DW, Pope CA, Xu X, Spendler JD, et al. "An Association Between Air Pollution and Mortality in Six U.S. Cities." N Engl J Med 1993 329:1753-59.) A 1995 study involving more than 550,000 residents of 151 U.S. metropolitan areas, in which subjects were followed for more than seven years, found a seventeen percent increase in mortality risk in areas with concentrations of small particles. (Pope CA, Thun MJ, Namboodiri MM, Dickery DW, et al. "Particulate Air Pollution as a Predictor of Mortality in a Prospective Study of U. S. Adults." Am J Respir Cir Med 1995; 151:699-74.)

72. "Breathtaking: Premature Mortality Due to Particulate Air Pollution in 239 American Cities," a report by the Natural Resource Defense Council, May 1996.

73. "Air pollution may trigger sudden deaths, Rise in particles alters heart rate, studies find," June 4, 2000; According to one groundbreaking study of 100 patients in Boston, conducted by the Harvard School of Public Health, when particle pollution increased, senior citizens with pacemakers suffered more arrhythmia. In another study, 26 senior citizens at a Baltimore nursing home wore heart monitors for three weeks. Their heart rate variability decreased on

and around days when particulate levels were higher, according to a study by the University of North Carolina and the EPA.

74. Texas Natural Resource Conservation Commission official publication "Natural Outlook," Spring 1997.

75. Texas Natural Resource Conservation Commission official publication "Natural Outlook," Spring 1997.

76. Texas Natural Resource Conservation Commission official publication "Natural Outlook," Spring 1997

77. Letter to Texas Natural Resource Conservation Commission from Jim Marston, Environmental Defense Fund, May 30, 1997. (www.edf.org).

78. Letter to Texas Natural Resource Conservation Commission from Jim Marston, Environmental Defense Fund (www.edf.org), May 30, 1997; Texas Natural Resource Conservation Commission official publication "Natural Outlook," Spring 1997.

79. Juan B. Elizondo Jr., "Emissions company, state settle lawsuit for $140 million," Associated Press, July 24, 1997; According to the news article, the company spent millions of dollars establishing 55 inspection stations in Dallas-Fort Worth, Houston-Galveston and Beaumont-Port Arthur, after federal officials had ordered emissions testing. Shortly after Tejas stations opened in January 1995, drivers protested the tests and Texas lawmakers reacted by killing the program. Another testing program that met less opposition was implemented. Tejas officials said killing the original program and the company's contract left them with $250 million in worthless testing stations. State District Judge Joseph Hart ordered the state to pay Tejas for abandoning the emissions testing program. He said the state had the right to change its mind, but couldn't leave Tejas with a worthless contract.

80. Public Employees for Environmental Responsibility, "Bush's quiet little war on the Texas environment: Assault on the regulatory front." (www.texpeer.org).

81. *Houston Chronicle*, "Bush defends clean-air stand / Cites call for automakers to produce cleaner-burning cars," December 18, 1999. *Houston Chronicle* Archives (www.chron.com/).

82. *Houston Chronicle*, "Bush touts cuts in plant pollution," November 16, 1999. *Houston Chronicle* Archives (www.chron.com/).

83. The term "grandfathered" means that a facility is exempted from having to obtain a state preconstruction permit, and from the associated requirement of best available air pollution control technology, public notice and a review of the facility's impact on public health. (From a background paper to the agency's Clean Air Responsibility Enterprise (CARE) Committee, which had been assigned the task of designing a voluntary program to reduce emissions from grandfathered facilities. Texas Natural Resource Conservation Commission, September 1997).

85. Texas Natural Resources Conservation Commission Air Emissions Inventory from Point Souce Database, made public in October, 1998; "Grandfathered Air Pollution, The Dirty Secret of Texas Industries" A report by the Galveston Houston Association for Smog Prevention (www.neosoft.com/~ghasp/) & the Lone Star Chapter of the Sierra Club (www.sierraclub.org/chapters/tx/), April 1998.

86."How the Grandfather Loophole Threatens Texas School Children," A report by the Sustainable Energy & Economic Development Coalition, 2nd Edition, 1999. (www.ion.com/~seed)

87. "How the Grandfather Loophole Threatens Texas School Children," A report by the Sustainable Energy & Economic Development Coalition, 2nd Edition, 1999. (www.ion.com/~seed)

88. In an effort to evaluate the influence that campaign contributions have on the legislative and regulatory processes, Public Research Works tracked four types of contributors: (1) the Political Action Committees (PACs) of the grandfathered companies and their parent companies; (2) company lobbyists who only work for a grandfathered or parent company; (3) "Hired Gun" lobbyists who work on contract for at least one grandfathered or parent companies, but who also work for other clients; and (4) one major industry association, the Texas Mid Continent Oil and Gas Association (TMOGA). Review Public the Research Works report at their Web site (www.foree.com/prw).

89. These meetings were secret because the general public and, specifically the public interest community, was never informed about these meetings. Only industry representatives, the TNRCC and the Governor's Office knew of these meetings – and they knew public interest organizations would have wanted to be involved. The memo to Governor Bush from his advisor who attended the meetings was identified as "intended to be privileged and confidential" and covered by the "Internal Memorandum Exception to the Texas Public Information Act."

90. Sustainable Energy and Economic Development Coalition obtained the records by using the Texas Open Records Law. (www.ion.com/~seed)

91. "Suit claims governor's office sat on pollution-plan records," article by Ralph Haurwitz, *Austin American Statesman* (1999), archives (www.austin 360.com/statesman); A lawsuit filed by the Sustainable Energy and Economic Development Coalition (www.ion.com/~seed) against Governor Bush alleged that some records believed to be in Governor's possession are being illegally withheld.

92. January 14, 1997 John Howard Memo "RE: Grandfathered Air Emission Sources" to Governor George W. Bush; The memo was "intended to be privileged and confidential" and covered by the "Internal Memorandum Exception to the Texas Public Information Act." The memo can be viewed on the Web site of Texas PEER: (www.txpeer.org).

93. November 14, 1997 "Confidential" memo re: "grandfathered facilities" from David Duncan to: JPILLIP, KMCCALLA, LGONZALE.

94. June 11, 1997 memo "RE: - Grandfathered Facilities in Texas" sent out by the Exxon and Marathon offices of V. G. Beghini and A. L. Condray to a "Distribution List" of 21 refinery managers, chief executive officers, and other top industry representatives. The memo states, "In early March, while discussing the National Ambient Air Quality Standards Issue with Governor Bush, he asked us to work with his office to develop the concepts of a voluntary program to permit grandfathered facilities in Texas. At his request, we have developed the concepts of a voluntary program. The process has now evolved to a point where we need to include other companies having significant grandfathered facilities to encourage their participation in developing this program."

95. April 25, 1997 Cover letter and memo from Governor Bush's environmental advisor John Howard, to TNRCC Commissioner Ralph Marquez conveying, "1st proposal from Exxon/Marathon" titled, "Permitting Grandfathered Facilities, Texas Voluntary Initiative."

96. June 23, 1997 Memo from Bernie Allen Jr. to John Barksdale re: "Grandfathered Meeting." The memo forwarded notes of the June 19, 1997 meeting taken by Jim Kennedy of DuPont.. The memo can be viewed on the Web site of Texas PEER: (www.txpeer.org).

97. John Howard's presence was noted in sign in sheets, and various memo's and meeting notes, according to Peter Altman, Director of the Sustainability Energy and Environment Coalition (SEED). SEED obtained the records by using the Texas Open Records Law and filed a lawsuit against Governor Bush

alleging that some records, believed to be in Governor's possession, are being illegally withheld.

98. June 23, 1997 Memo from Bernie Allen Jr. to John Barksdale re: "Grandfathered Meeting." The memo forwarded notes of the June 19, 1997 meeting taken by Jim Kennedy of DuPont.. The memo can be viewed on the Web site of Texas PEER: (www.txpeer.org).

99. June 23, 1997 Memo from Bernie Allen Jr. to John Barksdale re: "Grandfathered Meeting." The memo forwarded notes of the June 19, 1997 meeting taken by Jim Kennedy of DuPont..

100. June 23, 1997 Memo from Bernie Allen Jr. to John Barksdale re: "Grandfathered Meeting." The memo forwarded notes of the June 19, 1997 meeting taken by Jim Kennedy of DuPont..

101. June 23, 1997 Memo from Bernie Allen Jr. to John Barksdale re: "Grandfathered Meeting." The memo forwarded notes of the June 19,1997 meeting taken by Jim Kennedy of DuPont.

102. Texas Natural Resource Conservation Commission (TNRCC) 1997 Source Status Survey Report. This survey identified grandfathered facilities in Texas and the amounts of their criteria pollutants.

103. Research conducted by Texans for Public Justice www.onr.com/~tpj).. Contributions to both of Bush's gubernatorial campaigns totaled $4000. Maximum allowable individual contribution to Bush's Presidential Campaign was $1000 each.

104. Texans for Public Justice (www.onr.com/~tpj).

105. Documentation of Crown's violations and the amounts of pollution were obtained from Crown's own records and from the files of the Texas Natural Resource Conservation Commission and the Harris County Pollution Control Department. EPA Regional Administrator Greg Cooke wrote in a July 23, 1998 letter to the TNRCC, "Crown has a long history of both federal and state administrative enforcement actions for violations of air emission and equipment standards. Since early 1983, the TNRCC has attempted to bring Crown Central into compliance with these standards. Further, since 1986, Crown Central has violated sulfur dioxide standards and other emission limits."

106. Texans United Education Fund et. al. Vs. Crown Central Petroleum, H-97-2427 (S.D. Tex) This lawsuit was brought by Texans United, the Sierra Club, the Natural Resources Defense Council and several Pasadena families.

107. Allman, et al. vs. Crown Central Petroleum Corporation, et al., C.A. No. 97-39455 (District Court of Harris County, Texas) Several hundred residents and property owners near Crown suit accusing the refinery of disrupting their daily life and health through negligent operations.

108. On February 5, 1996, Crown forced 252 employees, all OCAW members, to leave their jobs at the refinery and locked the gate behind them. Crown's lock-out was an attempt force employees to accept major concessions during contract negotiations. Crown replaced the experienced union employees with temporary contract employees. Since the lock-out, these contract employees have been operating the plant. After the lock-out, the hours of pollution violations and the amount of pollution increased.

109. Texas Natural Resource Conservation Commission News Release of August 1998 referred to the $1,055,425 penalty assessed against Crown as the "largest in Texas history for air quality violations."

110. "To Little-To Late," a study released in November of 1998 by the Environmental Defense Fund. The report can be viewed at EDF's Web site: (www.edf.org).

111. Texas Natural Resource Conservation Commission News Release of August 1998 referred to the $1,055,425 penalty assessed against Crown as the "largest in Texas history for air quality violations." However, the fine did not take into account Crown's economic benefit from the years of violations. Because of this failure, the TNRCC was sued in state court by Texans United and a formal civil rights complaint was filed against the TNRCC with the EPA by Texans United and the Sierra Club.

112. "Texas needs to quit coddling polluter," *Austin American Statesman*, April 14, 1999 (www.austin360.com/statesman); Clean Air, Legislature should close loophole for older plants, " *Dallas Morning News*, 1999, (www.dallasnews.com/); "Clamp Down on Polluters", *El Paso Times*, 1999 (www.elpasotimes.com/)

113. Senate Research Center analysis of Senate Bill 766. Section 12 of the legislation "Prohibits the commission from initiating enforcement actions against a person who files an application for a certain permit on or before August 31, 2001." This provision prevented the state environmental agency from bringing enforcement action against companies that, illegally operated their facilities without a required permit.

114. Reported by Alan Miller, *Los Angeles Times*, "Texas Corporate Interests Financed Bulk of Bush Races," July 14, 1999. Archives (www.latimes.com/)

115. Susan B. Glasser and John Mintz, *Washington Post*, "Bush Capitol Plan to Woo Big Business; First He Wins Over Trade Group Chiefs," August 1, 1999. Archives (www.washingtonpost.com)

116. Public Research Works (www.foree.com/prw) and Center for Responsive Politics (www.crp.org/).

117. Emissions data identifying grandfathered facilities and their pollution amounts is available at TNRCC's Web Site (www.tnrcstate.tx.us/).

118. Emissions data identifying grandfathered facilities and their pollution amounts is available at TNRCC's Web Site (www.tnrcstate.tx.us/).

119. Public Research Works (www.foree.com/prw) and Center for Responsive Politics (www.crp.org/).

120. "Breathtaking: Premature Mortality Due to Particulate Air Pollution in 239 American Cities", a report by the Natural Resource Defense Council., May 1996.

121. "Assessment of the Health Benefits of Improving Air Quality in Houston Texas," April 1999, Sonoma Technology.

122. "Out of Breath: Adverse Health Effects Associated with Ozone in the Eastern Untied Sates," October 1999, Abt Associates Inc.

123. Brochure by Government Institutes Division, ABS Group Inc, The brochure advertised workshops for industry representatives to be held in October 2000.

124. "The Privileged Class: Bush pushes Secrecy for Environmental Audits," Public Employees for Environmental Responsibility.    K. Goleman acknowledged his role in Payne, Chris, "Controversial law employed by UTA: Cover of secrecy allowed for audits," Fort Worth Star Telegram, February 16, 1996. (www..star-telegram.com/)

125. "The Privileged Class: Bush pushes Secrecy for Environmental Audits," Public Employees for Environmental Responsibility, references TNRCC Environmental Audit Log Computer printout received from the agency October 29, 1999.

126. Bush fund-raising totals are derived from a database of Texas lobby donors compiled by Public Research Works. Since these amounts only include donations of $1,000 and up, this total is likely an understatement.

127. "The Privileged Class: Bush pushes Secrecy for Environmental Audits," Public Employees for Environmental Responsibility, quotes and paraphrases of positions of proponents and opponents of the legislation were transcribed from tapes of a 3/21/95 House Environmental Regulations Committee hearing.

128. "The Privileged Class: Bush pushes Secrecy for Environmental Audits," Public Employees for Environmental Responsibility. Unattributed criticisms of or arguments for the law were paraphrased from House Research Organization, Bill Analysis: HB 2473, Chisum et al., April 25, 1995..

129. Letter from Texas Natural Resources and Conservation Commission Chairman Barry McBee to EPA Assistant Administrator Steven Herman, March 17, 1997.

130. "The Privileged Class: Bush pushes Secrecy for Environmental Audits," Public Employees for Environmental Responsibility references a September 22, 1997 interview with attorney Rick Lowerre.

131. "The Privileged Class: Bush pushes Secrecy for Environmental Audits," Public Employees for Environmental Responsibility.

132. "The Privileged Class: Bush pushes Secrecy for Environmental Audits," Public Employees for Environmental Responsibility. Source of information on audits and disclosures by company is TNRCC's Environmental Audit Log, 10-1-99 as referenced in Analysis of Bush contributors performed by Public Employees for Environmental Responsibility and Public Research Works.

133. Payne, Chris, "Controversial law employed by UTA: Cover of secrecy allowed for audits," *Fort Worth Star Telegram*, February 16, 1996, (www.star-telegram,com/).

134 Public Employees for Environmental Responsibility references TNRCC FY 1996-97 budget as approved by the 1995 legislature.

135. Public Employees for Environmental Responsibility references The Council of State Governments, Resource Guide to State Environmental Management, 1st, 4th, and 5th Editions. (Texas uses a two year budget cycle). (www.txpeer.org)

136. August 30, 2000 interview with Neil Carmen, Ph.D., a former inspector with the Texas Air Control Board who became the Clean Air Director Lone Star Chapter of the Sierra Club.

137. TNRCC's John Young's August 28, 1996 response to a July 7, 1996 inquiry from TNRCC's Zoe Rascoe.

138. "TNRCC Enforcement: Records or Rhetoric," Texas Center for Policy Studies, December 1996. (www.texascenter.org/)

139. Texas Health and Safety Code

140. After TNRCC inspectors discovered a long list of environmental violations at Exxon's Baytown facility a civil penalty of $847,460 was recommended. The TNRCC "negotiated" with Exxon for almost a year and a half before finally reaching an out-of-court settlement in April of 1995 which allowed Exxon to pay only $460,000 to the state and to spend another $400,000 on "supplemental environmental projects (SEPs)." Exxon was allowed to choose its own SEPs, which included projects in the community already supported by Exxon. Texans United, Baytown residents, the County Attorney and the labor union representing Exxon employees, all supported a plan where some of the penalty money would go to the County environmental agency for monitoring equipment that was needed to investigate air pollution complaints. Instead, the TNRCC allowed Exxon to buy real estate." The real estate, with title held in Exxon's name and for Exxon's use, was to be used as a "greenbelt." Penalty funds were also  spent on an industry sponsored air monitoring program that did not respond to citizen complaints. Exxon did use a small portion of the fine to renovate an old bowling alley into what it called an "environmental education center."

141. House Bill 2776, was passed by the Legislature and signed into law by Governor Bush in the 75th (1997) Texas Legislative session.

142. "Superfund a Super Deal for Texas Polluters," Public Employees for Environmental Responsibility references the Recommendations of the Fund 550 Workgroup, August 1996. Page 1. Of the recommendations mention that the executive director of the TNRCC instigated the workgroup. (www.txpeer.org)

143. "Superfund a Super Deal for Texas Polluters," Public Employees for Environmental Responsibility references Brown's comment being transcribed from a tape of the Senate Natural Resources Committee hearing on May 13, 1997. (www.txpeer.org)

144. August 2000 interview with Neil Carman, Clean Air Director of the Lone Star Chapter of the Sierra Club; Interview with Sierra Club Director Ken Kramer referenced in "Superfund a Super Deal for Texas Polluters," Public Employees for Environmental Responsibility (www.txpeer.org).

145. Interview with TNRCC Superfund division employee of December 14, 1999 referenced in "Superfund a Super Deal for Texas Polluters," Public Employees for Environmental Responsibility (www.txpeer.org).

146. House Research Organization Bill Analysis, HB 2776, May 5, 1997. (www.capitol.state.tx.us)

147. "Organic Toxicants and pathogens in Sewage Sludge and Their Environmental Effects," JG Babish, DJ Lisk, GS Stoewsand, and C Wilkinson, A Special Report of the Subcommittee on Organics in Sludge, Cornell university, College of Agriculture and Life Sciences, December 1981.

148. Interview with Bill Addington of Save Sierra Blanca and the Sierra Blanca Legal Defense Fund, August 28, 2000. (www.compassionate.org/sbldf)

149. Allen R. Myerson, "Flood of Money Wins an Uneasy Home in Texas for New York City Waste", The *New York Times*, July 17, 1995; and "Stink Over Sludge", Kevin Flynn and Michael Moss, New York Newsday, August 2, 1994; "Ex mob boss testimony muddies sludge company," *El Paso Times*, June 19,1992.

150. Interview with Bill Addington of Save Sierra Blanca and the Sierra Blanca Legal Defense Fund, August 28, 2000. (www.compassionate.org/sbldf)

151. "At their disposal West Texas Residents object to playing host to relocated NY sludge, *"Dallas Morning News* (www.dallasnews.com/) May 27, 1992. Merco's application was submitted and shepherded through the agency by former Texas Water Commissioner and Austin lobbyist Cliff Johnson. Despite a backlog of at least 60 applications -- and a review process that had previously taken four to six months, the agency approved Merco's contract in just 23 days. A Water Commission official. admitted that "Most of them are taking months. "

152. "Little town even tops El Paso, Just 1 donor puts Sierra Blanca ahead," *El Paso Times*, Monday March 14, 1994. (www.elpasotimes.com/).

153. Telephone interview with Bill Addington, Sierra Blanca Legal Defense Fund., August 30, 2000. (www.compassionate.org/sbldf).

154. "Earthly odor" quote from interview with Bill of the Sierra Blanca Legal Defense Fun (www.compassionate.org/sbldf)..

155. Texas Administrative Code 30 (C): Prior to any off-site transportation or on-site use or disposal of any sewage sludge generated at a wastewater treatment facility, the chief certified operator of the wastewater treatment facility or other responsible official who manages the processes to significantly reduce pathogens at the wastewater treatment facility for the permittee, shall certify that the sewage sludge underwent at least the minimum operational requirements necessary in order to meet one of the Processes to Significantly Reduce Pathogens. The acceptable processes and the minimum operational and record-keeping requirements shall be in accordance with established U.S. Environmental        Protection        Agency        final        guidance. (www.compassionate.org/sbldf).

156. Telephone interview with Bill Addington, a third generation   Sierra Blanca      resident      and      business      owner,      August      30,      2000. (www.compassionate.org/sbldf).

157. The Texas Low-Level Radioactive Disposal Compact Consent Act. Established that a total of 50 million dollars in construction fees would come to Texas from Main and Vermont. (www.compassionate.org/sbldf).

158. "Richards: Border won't be hazardous dumping ground," *El Paso Times*, April 11, 1992.

159. The Texas Low-Level Radioactive Waste Disposal Authority license application, noted that there were 64 earthquakes with magnitudes of 3.0 or greater within 200 miles of the proposed site in the previous 70 years. (www.compassionate.org/sbldf)

160. Sierra Blanca Legal Defense Fund "Congressional Alert," March 13, 1998.   The nuclear industry's "Compact Coalition" was a lobby group comprised of the Texas Low Level Radioactive Waste Disposal Authority, Governor Bush's Office of State-Federal Relations, the nuclear utilities of Texas, Maine, and Vermont, and other supporters of nuclear dumping in Texas. Together they had poured hundreds of thousands of dollars into lobbying since the legislation's original defeat in 1995. (www.compassionate.org/sbldf)

161. Sierra Blanca Legal Defense Fund "Congressional Alert," March 13, 1998 (www.compassionate.org/sbldf).   Low-level waste from nuclear power plants includes control roods from the reactor core, poison curtains from the reactor core and irradiated fuel pool, resins, slugs, and filters (which trap pieces of fuel roods that have deteriorated while in the reactor.  Level waste also includes the entire plant itself upon decommissioning.  This was significant because Maine was in the process of decommissioning its nuclear power plant.  "Just The Facts," from the Sierra Blanca Legal Defense Fund, wastes include elements

like plutonium (hazardous for 500,000 years), iodine-129 (hazardous for 160 million years), strontium-90 (hazardous for 300 years), and nickel-59 (hazardous for 760,000 years). The "acceptable body dose" of plutonium is one millionth of a gram, because of its cancer-causing properties.

162. "West Texas Notes," *Associated Press Wire Service*, February 5, 1998. Bush said. "As I told the Ambassador [from Mexico], much of the discussion is about disposal of, for example, X-rays. And there's tons of X-rays piled up in El Paso hospitals as we speak today," he said. "This is low-level radioactive waste. This is not high-powered plutonium." (www.compassionate.org/sbldf).

163. Statement of Pete Duarte, CEO of Thomason Hospital (El Paso County Hospital). Referenced in (www,txpeer.org); (www.compassionate.org/sbldf).

164. State-by-State Assessment of Low-Level Radioactive Wastes received at Commercial Dumpsites 1990-1994, US Department of Energy, National Low Level Waste Management Program, Idaho Falls, Idaho.

165. "U.S. House Passes Compact Bill," Sierra Blanca Legal Defense Fund News Release of Oct 7, 1997 (www.compassionate.org/sbldf).

166. "U.S. House Passes Compact Bill," Sierra Blanca Legal Defense Fund News Release of Oct 7, 1997 (www.compassionate.org/sbldf). The Maine Yankee Nuclear Plant was permanently shut down and the Maine Yankee Board of Directors decided to dismantle the power plant and dump it immediately. "We believe that the Texas facility is unlikely to be in existence or ready to take waste when we most need it," stated Maine Yankee Board Chairman David Flanagan. "Moreover," he said, "its comparative cost will be much higher than the available alternatives." The statements were made in a October 3, 1997 letter to Texas Rep. Bonilla.

167. The letter, which Bush signed on September 23, 1997, was used to build Congressional support for the Texas dumpsite plan that was clearly in trouble.

168. Conducted by Bannon Research for Public Citizen September 29-October 3, 1994. The margin of error is 4.9%.

169. Analysis provided by Bill Addington and the Sierra Blanca Legal Defense Fund Web Site (www.compassionate.org/sbldf).

170. Texas Natural Resource Conservation Commission files on TXI. Also See (www.cement kiln.com/downwinders)

171. August 27, 2000 interview with Jim Schermbeck of the organization Downwinders at Risk; According to several representatives of the citizen

organization, the Commissioner's statement was reported in *Dallas Morning News* article. The Downwinders Web site is: (www.cementkiln.com/downwinders).

172. American Lung Association of Texas report: Evaluation of The Screening Risk Analysis for the Texas Industries (TXI) Facility in Midlothian, Texas, written by TNRCC. May 1, 1996.

173. American Lung Association of Texas report: Evaluation of The Screening Risk Analysis for the Texas Industries (TXI) Facility in Midlothian, Texas, written by TNRCC. Executive Summary, May 1, 1996. Also see (www.cementkiln.com/downwinders).

174. American Lung Association of Texas report: Evaluation of The Screening Risk Analysis for the Texas Industries (TXI) Facility in Midlothian, Texas, written by TNRCC. Executive Summary, May 1, 1996. Also see (www.cementkiln.com/downwinders).

175. American Lung Association of Texas report: Evaluation of The Screening Risk Analysis for the Texas Industries (TXI) Facility in Midlothian, Texas, written by TNRCC. Executive Summary, May 1, 1996. Also see (www.cementkiln.com/downwinders).

176. American Lung Association of Texas report: Evaluation of The Screening Risk Analysis for the Texas Industries (TXI) Facility in Midlothian, Texas, written by TNRCC. Executive Summary, May 1, 1996. Also see (www.cementkiln.com/downwinders).

177. American Lung Association of Texas report: Evaluation of The Screening Risk Analysis for the Texas Industries (TXI) Facility in Midlothian, Texas, written by TNRCC. Executive Summary, May 1, 1996. Also see (www.cementkiln.com/downwinders).

178. American Lung Association of Texas report: Evaluation of The Screening Risk Analysis for the Texas Industries (TXI) Facility in Midlothian, Texas, written by TNRCC. Executive Summary, May 1, 1996. Also see (www.cementkiln.com/downwinders).

179. American Lung Association of Texas report: Evaluation of The Screening Risk Analysis for the Texas Industries (TXI) Facility in Midlothian, Texas, written by TNRCC. Executive Summary, May 1, 1996. Also see (www.cementkiln.com/downwinders).

180. Interview with Jim Schermbeck of the organization Downwinders at Risk, August 27, 2000. The organization analyzed all industrial emissions from sources in the Dallas-Fort Worth area. (www.cementkiln.com/downwinders)

181. Texans for Public Justice Campaign Contribution Data Base. (www.tpj.org/)

182. "Local Control"—Texas Style," Public Employees for Environmental Responsibility (www.txpeer.org) references *Austin American Statesman* article of April 29, 1995. (www.austin 360.com/statesman)

183. "Local Control"—Texas Style," Public Employees for Environmental Responsibility (www.txpeer.org) references *Austin American Statesman*, October 12, 1994 news article. Archives (www.austin360.com/statesman).

.184 "Local Control"—Texas Style," Public Employees for Environmental Responsibility (www.txpeer.org) references *Austin American Statesman*, April 29, 1995 news article. Archives (www.austin.360.com/statesman).

185. Prior to the passage of SB1017, cities over 5,000 population were authorized to extend water quality regulations to their extraterritorial jurisdiction in order to prevent the pollution of their water supply.

186. Summary information from the Texas Legislative House Research Organization

187. TNRCC memo referenced in "Local Control"—Texas Style," Public Employees for Environmental Responsibility (www.txpeer.org); *Austin American Statesman*, April 26, 1995. Archives (www.austin.360.com/statesman).

188 Texas Supreme Court Case 98-0685, June 15, 2000; Interview with Attorney Bill Bunch, Executive Director of the Save Our Springs Alliance, September 13, 2000.

189. "Local Control"—Texas Style," Public Employees for Environmental Responsibility (www.txpeer.org)

190. *Austin American Statesman*, March 25, 1995 news article referenced in "Local Control"—Texas Style," Public Employees for Environmental Responsibility (www.txpeer.org); *Austin American Statesman* archives (www.austin 360.com/statesman).

.191 Interview with Attorney Bill Bunch, Executive Director of the Save Our Springs Alliance, September 13, 2000.

192. "Texas Isn't Keeping Up with Its Stewardship Role," *Austin American Statesman* Editorial, May 14, 2000. Archives (www.austin 360.com/statesman).

193. Texas Parks and Wildlife Department News, "1997 In Review-TPW's Top 10 News Stories," December 22, 1997.

194. Texas Parks and Wildlife Department, 1998, 1999, 2000 Infrastructure Report and Facility Repair Budgets.

195. "Auditor's Report Cites Need for More State Park Funding", Texas Parks and Wildlife Department News Release, Oct. 5, 1998.

196. "TPW Requesting Additional $35 Million for Critical Needs," Texas Parks and Wildlife Department News Release, March 8, 1999.

197. Richard Heath, "Texas parks doing more with less, but need more," *Houston Chronicle* (www.chron.com/), November 9, 1998; William McKenzie, "Texas should recognize value of parks," *Dallas Morning News* (www.dallas news.com/), April 6,1999.

198. *Austin American Statesman*: "Texas is "Tight-Fisted" When It Comes to Public Land Holdings," May 14, 2000. Archives (www.austin360.com/)

199. Sunset Advisory Commission Staff Report on Texas Parks and Wildlife Department, Page 21, April, 2000.

200. "Texas Isn't Keeping Up with Its Stewardship Role," *Austin American Statesman* Editorial, May 14, 2000. (www.austin360.com/statesman)

201. Public Research Works (www..foree.com/prw) and Center for Responsive Politics

202. "Sierra Club Criticizes Governor Bush's Attempts to "Greenwash" His Record on Land Conservation" Sierra Club News Release, April 11, 2000. (cwww.sierralub.org)

203. Quotes from June 2000 Campaign Speech available on Bush Web site (www.georgewbush.com).

204. Governor Bush's efforts to seek public input and participation in the development major pieces of environmental legislation, such as that related to audit privilege and air pollution from "grandfathered" industries, have involved committees stacked with special interest (industry) representatives and little or no representation from public interest groups. The legislative Sunset Commission also found during Governor Bush's administration, that the

Commissioners of the Texas Parks and Wildlife Department made decisions without adequate opportunity for public input. The opportunity for public comment occurred after Commissioners met in committee where preliminary votes were taken and decisions were made.

205. "Texas Gov. George W. Bush is promising "sweeping changes" in the Clinton administration's environmental policies, especially in the Pacific Northwest," *the Seattle Post-Intelligencer*, June 2000.

206. News Release, Sierra Club Criticizes Governor Bush's Attempts to "Greenwash" His Record on Land Conservation Tuesday, April 11, 2000. (www.sierraclub.org/chapters/tx/).

207. 1994 State Republican Party Platform" pp. 5-6 as referenced in "Privatizing Texas Public Parks - Public Land, Private Profit, Public Employees for Environmental Responsibility (www.txpeer.org).

208. Quotes from June 2000 Campaign Speech. (www.georgewbush.com)

209. "Major changes not far away for Fort Davis and Big Bend," *Davis County Mountain Dispatch*, Oct. 14, 1999. "Privatizing Texas Public Parks - Public Land, Private Profit," Public Employees for Environmental Responsibility (www.txpeer.org).

210. Texas Parks and Wildlife Department Economic and Environmental Feasibility Study: Request for Proposals. Referenced in "Privatizing Texas Public Parks - Public Land, Private Profit," Public Employees for Environmental Responsibility (www.txpeer.org).

211. "Privatizing Texas Public Parks - Public Land, Private Profit," Public Employees for Environmental Responsibility (www.txpeer.org).

212. "Privatizing Texas Public Parks - Public Land, Private Profit," Public Employees for Environmental Responsibility (www.txpeer.org).

213. "Texas PEER Uncovers Misuse of Federal Funds by Texas Parks and Wildlife Department: Criminal Complaint Filed," Public Employees for Environmental Responsibility Web site: (www.txpeer.org).

214. Blakeslee, N., "Misadventures with the New Texas Naturalists", Texas Observer, August 14, 1998, (www.texasobserver.org/).

215. "Park Visitation Access Restricted During Special Hunts," Texas Parks and Wildlife Department News, Sept. 13, 1999.

216. "Texas Gov. George W. Bush is promising "sweeping changes" in the Clinton administration's environmental policies, especially in the Pacific Northwest," the Seattle Post-Intelligencer, June 2000.

217. TNRCC Executive Director Dan Pearson's February 6, 1998 letter to EPA Region 6.

218. Campaign funding research conducted by Public Research Works (www.foree.com/prw).

219. The hearing took place in the 250th District Court in the Travis County Court House on August 29, 2000. The ruling was issued by Judge John K. Dietz. The lawsuit is styled, "Texans United Education Fund et al. Vs. George W. Bush and the Department of Public Safety (DPS), Cause No. 99-10051. The judge reaffirmed his decision at a subsequent hearing on September 5, 2000The lawsuit against Bush and the DPS was filed in August of 1999 by citizens who were arrested and jailed for peacefully protesting against Governor Bush's Environmental Policies on four different occasions in early 1999.

220. Deposition of Governor's Office employee Shirley Green, Texans United Education Fund et. al. Vs. George W. Bush and the Department of Public Safety (DPS), Cause No. 99-10051.

221. "Bush 'backer' makes point about protest," *Dallas Morning News*, April 22, 1999. (www.dallasnews.com/)

222. "Texans United Education Fund et. al. Vs. George W. Bush and the Department of Public Safety (DPS), Cause No. 99-10051."